TCHAIKOVSKY

HIS LIFE AND WORKS

PETER ILICH TCHAIKOVSKY.

TCHAIKOVSKY

HIS LIFE AND WORKS, WITH EXTRACTS
FROM HIS WRITINGS, AND THE
DIARY OF HIS TOUR
ABROAD IN 1888

BY

ROSA NEWMARCH

GREENWOOD PRESS, PUBLISHERS
NEW YORK

Originally published in 1900
by John Lane, the Bodley Head, N.Y.

First Greenwood Reprinting, 1969

Library of Congress Catalogue Card Number 69-14011

PRINTED IN UNITED STATES OF AMERICA

TO

HENRY J. WOOD

WHO HAS HELPED TO REALISE

SO MANY OF TCHAIKOVSKY'S MASTERPIECES

AND TO HIS WIFE

Preface

SIX years have now elapsed since Tchaikovsky's death, and as yet no really adequate biography has appeared, either in Russia or abroad. The authorised *Life and Letters* has long been expected in vain. Probably the difficulty of selecting from such a vast mass of correspondence — Tchaikovsky's letters are said to be numbered by thousands — is the chief reason for the delay in publication. Meanwhile the public interest, especially in England, is steadily increasing, and almost every scrap of information concerning the composer of "The Pathetic" Symphony is eagerly sought after. In the absence of anything more complete and authoritative I venture to offer this volume to the admirers of Tchaikovsky's works.

In 1897 I published in *The Musician* a series of papers upon Tchaikovsky based upon a little volume of personal reminiscences by M. N. Kashkin,[1] one

[1] *Reminiscences of Peter Ilich Tchaikovsky*, by N. Kashkin, Moscow, 1897 (P. Jurgenson).

of the Professors of the Moscow Conservatoire, and a friend and colleague of the composer. These papers, which I have been repeatedly asked to reprint, form the first part of the present volume. They have been almost entirely rewritten, and supplemented by a considerable amount of new information derived from other and more recent sources.

In 1898 appeared *The Collected Writings of Tchaikovsky*, edited, with a preface, by the well-known Russian critic G. Laroche. From this book I made a collection of extracts showing the composer's musical tastes and sympathies, and these papers appeared in the *Musical Standard* under the title, " Tchaikovsky as a Musical Critic." The fact that they were very well noticed in several Russian papers, notably the *Moscow Viedomosti*, induced me to reprint them here, with two additional chapters dealing with Tchaikovsky's attitude towards Russian music. Later on, at the suggestion of Mr. C. A. Barry, I undertook to translate the diary of Tchaikovsky's tour abroad in 1888, now published for the first time in English. And so the book grew to its present size.

No one can be more conscious than myself of its shortcomings, and of the patchy nature of its construction. If it has not been altogether a case of making bricks without straw, at least the straw has been scattered on the four winds of journalism and has had to be gathered up in the by-ways of Russian musical literature.

My thanks are due to the editors of *The Musician* and the *Musical Standard* for their courteous permission to reprint such matter as has already appeared in those papers. I must also express my gratitude to M. Kashkin and M. Laroche, from whose works I have quoted freely ; and particularly to M. Berezovsky, whose excellent article on Tchaikovsky contains invaluable information. To the composer's brother, M. Modeste Tchaikovsky, I am indebted for permission to republish the Diary of 1888 ; while M. P. Jurgenson has kindly supplied me with the facsimile from the score of the *Overture 1812*. Last, but not least, I have to thank M. Vladimir Stassov, whose ready help and sympathy first enabled me to undertake the study of Russian art.

TCHAIKOVSKY

AMONG the leaders of the New School of music in Russia Tchaikovsky occupies an exceptional place, as one who, while strongly attracted by the forward movements of his time, was restrained by his special training from acknowledging complete allegiance to the nationalist party. His character was essentially Russian, and his tendencies the liberating tendencies of the generation to which he belonged ; but his musical education was cosmopolitan, and the teachers whom he most reverenced leaned towards tradition and authority. He was not, like Glinka, or, in a less degree, like Rimsky - Korsakov, consecrated to the service of nationality. In his heart a follower of Liszt, in his intellectual conscience an adherent of Classicism, Tchaikovsky composed under the sway of two conflicting influences, neither of which was strong enough to efface for long his own intense personality. Thus throughout his work we find a lack of unity which baffles dogmatic criticism, and compels us to seek in the character of the man, rather than in his theories, the interpretation of all he has expressed in music. This susceptibility to the antagonistic currents of thought and feeling which surrounded him is not altogether a fault in Tchaikovsky. On the contrary, it has lent to his music qualities of pliancy, variety, and eclecticism which have proved sources of charm and attraction. It distinguishes him from most of his contemporaries, and places him in the sharpest contrast alike to Wagner, whose militant energies forced a new channel of their own, and to Brahms, whose work was mainly accomplished under the influence of a single dominant idea ●

> that Freedom slowly broadens down
> From precedent to precedent.

Even if we admit that this division of thought and emotion is a source of weakness in Tchaikovsky, we must also acknowledge that it has its element of popularity. At a time when the entire world of art is divided upon questions of law and liberty, this subjective confession of unsettled faith and dual allegiance puts him in closer touch with his own generation, though it may weaken his hold upon succeeding ones.

Another source alike of weakness and popularity in Tchaikovsky's music is his sympathy with the *maladie du siècle*; his command of every note in the gamut of melancholy. "A poet of one mood in all his lays," his monotony of pessimism, though it must at times weary the sane-minded individual, seems to engage the public and draw them to him most persistently in his moods of blackest despair. In this respect, foreigners consider his music typically Russian ; a view not entirely just to Russian art as a whole, which is far too vigorous and healthy a growth to remain continuously under the sway of one emotional influence. Nor is Tchaikovsky's melancholy of that particular type which we associate with the Russian character : that sober, grey-tinted, resigned pessimism which is a part of the Russian nature rather than a mood, and is best exemplified in the poems of Nekrasov. Tchaikovsky's emotional and romantic despair seems to belong to other times and other lands. It echoes Chateaubriand and Byron, not Gogol and Tourgeniev.

To say that Tchaikovsky is the most accessible and the best known among Russian composers is by no means to say that he is the greatest. Unlike the majority of the school to which he—in part—belongs, he did not in his lifetime disdain popularity, and has reaped his reward in a wider fame and a stronger sway over the public taste. Setting aside his natural dislike of public appearances, he was the first of the Russians to travel in his own goods, if I may use so commercial a simile. Partly for this reason, and partly because his music possesses in the highest degree those qualities of highly-wrought emotion and brilliant workmanship which are always the first to awaken a sympathetic echo, he has made a greater impression than any of his compatriots. It is the fashion to praise Tchaikovsky for having cast aside so much of his national peculiarities as impeded his progress towards the goal of fame. This action was not so much a matter of conviction as of temperament and the circumstances of his education. It was easier for him to drop the Slav than for many of his fellow-workers. Fortunately, too, he could not altogether get rid of that imperishable fibre of race to which he owes so much that is interesting and original. There are few compensations for the sale of our birthright. Nationality in art may have its narrowing results, but the lasting influences in music, as in literature, have never been effected by the *dépaysés*.

I do not deny that Tchaikovsky possesses many of the virtues of a master artist, but we shall miss much if we let our appreciation of Russian music stop short at his works alone. In each member of the group which he partially represents, there is some individual charm or gift, some concentration of artistic purpose to a definite aim, in the highest degree interesting to the student. The wisest will let Tchaikovsky's achievement—with which we are beginning to be familiar—serve as an elucidation of the great national movement which lay behind it, and as an introduction to the music—less stirring perhaps, but not less worthy—of his immediate predecessors.

I

Peter Ilich Tchaikovsky was born 7th May 1840, at Votinsk, in the government of Viatka. His father

was employed there as a mining engineer, but later on
he moved to St. Petersburg, where he was appointed
Director of the Technological Institute. The boy
was educated at the School of Jurisprudence, and afterwards obtained a post in the Ministry of Justice.

Like most of the Russian composers, Tchaikovsky
began his musical career as an amateur. Launched
upon the society of the capital as an average youth
of fashion, his musical gifts won him considerable
popularity. At evening parties he shone in such
pieces as Döhler's *Nocturne in D flat* and
Weber's *Invitation à la Valse*; but he had higher
ideals than these. The atmosphere of the School
of Jurisprudence was decidedly musical, thanks to
the influence of its patron Prince Oldenburgsky.
Tchaikovsky's most intimate school friend was the
future author Apukhtin, a young man of cultivated
and artistic tastes, who was passionately fond of Italian
music. The two friends spent their free evenings
at the opera, and most of their leisure moments in
discussing their favourite art. Apukhtin refers to this
in one of his poems, dedicated to Tchaikovsky :—

> Do you remember how you used to drown
> Your soul in art, forget this world of men ?
> And how we dreamt of some ideal renown,
> For Music was our worshipped idol then,
> And Life a fleeting dream to us . . .

But in spite of this enthusiasm for music, it is doubtful
if Tchaikovsky had any serious thoughts of it as a
profession when first he took up his duties in the

Ministry of Justice. It would certainly have been considered *infra dig.* in the official circles in which he moved, besides which, it was imperative that he should begin to earn a livelihood as soon as possible. A trifling circumstance first started him upon the path that was destined eventually to become a triumphal way. Tchaikovsky had a cousin in the Mounted Grenadiers, who was also an amateur performer and a friendly rival at social evenings. One day, having met at the house of a mutual friend, they began to discuss musical questions. "Among other things," to relate the story in Tchaikovsky's own words, "my cousin said it was possible to modulate from one key to another without using more than three chords. This excited my curiosity, and to my astonishment I found that he improvised whatever modulations I suggested, even from quite extraneous keys." Tchaikovsky was piqued by this show of superior knowledge. "I asked him where he picked this up, and discovered that there were classes in connection with the Musical Society where one might learn all this wisdom."

Tchaikovsky lost no time in joining these classes, which were held at the Michailovsky Palace ; but, says Kashkin, he showed so little inclination for serious work that he was at first regarded as an incorrigible dilettante. Nevertheless, about this time he began to feel a strong impulse towards music as a vocation. But besides the question of means, he was lacking in self-confidence. In December 1861, he wrote to his sister : "I told you I was studying the theory of

music with considerable success. It is generally
agreed that with my uncommon talents (I hope you
will not take this for mere boasting) it would be a
pity not to try my luck in this career. I am only
afraid of a want of purpose; perhaps idleness may
take possession of me and I may not persevere. You
know I have power and capacity, but I am ailing
with your malady, which is called 'fragmentariness,'
and if I do not become enthusiastic over a thing I
am easily done for."

For some months Tchaikovsky remained in this
vacillating frame of mind. Without actually throw-
ing over his official duties he entered the Conservatoire, and was placed under Zaremba in the class for
counterpoint.

Anton Rubinstein often attended the harmony
classes at the Conservatoire to examine the work of
the students. Struck by the ability, and also by the
carelessness, of Tchaikovsky's exercises, he called him
aside after class, and spoke to him with such combined
charm and severity that the Laodicean mood vanished
for ever. Rubinstein's appeal irrevocably decided
Tchaikovsky's destiny, and henceforward he cherished
an adoration for the man who had pointed out his
true vocation. He now resigned his official appoint-
ment, withdrew from fashionable society, and devoted
himself entirely to the study of music. It is recorded
of Ilia Muromets—that popular hero of Russian folk-
lore—that he sat out the first thirty years of his life in
complete inactivity. Once roused from his lethargy,
however, his strength was as the strength of ten, and

his deeds of prowess unparalleled. Tchaikovsky might have taken this old hero for his model, he now proved himself so full of unsuspected energy and ambition.

"Tchaikovsky worked in an astonishing way," said Rubinstein, speaking of his pupil to Kashkin in later years. "Once, at the composition class, I set him to write out contrapuntal variations on a given theme, and I mentioned that in this class of work not only quality but *quantity* was of importance. I thought perhaps he would write about a dozen variations. But not at all. At the next class I received over two hundred. To examine all these," Rubinstein concluded, with a bland smile, "would have taken me more time than it took him to write them." Tchaikovsky, on leaving the Conservatoire some three years later, received a silver medal for his diploma work — a cantata for solo, chorus, and orchestra, the text from Schiller's *Ode to Joy*. With regard to this work, it is interesting to know that the composer himself did not look upon it by any means as a weak or immature effort, and would gladly have seen it published, or at least re-performed.

In 1863 Tchaikovsky began to study orchestration in Rubinstein's class. Rubinstein, as a composer, wrote only for the modern orchestra, while retaining at the same time the greatest reverence for the works of the old classical writers. He impressed these views upon his pupil, and made him adopt the habit of thinking and writing in the language of the modern orchestra from the beginning of his career.

Besides the piano, Tchaikovsky studied the flute and the organ. Rubinstein helped him to earn a living by recommending him as a teacher and accompanist. In the latter capacity he frequently attended the musical evenings of the Grand Duchess Helena Paulovna. At the Conservatoire he became intimate with his fellow-student Laroche, who exercised an important influence upon his future life.

Tchaikovsky now came to be regarded, both by masters and students, as a young man of very great promise. In 1864-65, Laroche — who afterwards became one of the foremost musical critics in Russia —wrote to Kashkin in Moscow of Tchaikovsky's excellent qualities, and pointed him out as "the future star of Russian music." Since 1863 harmony classes had been held in Moscow in connection with a branch of the Russian Musical Society, under the management of Nicholas Rubinstein. Rubinstein had neither time nor inclination to devote himself to the teaching of theory, and in view of the opening of the Moscow Conservatoire, in 1866, it was thought necessary to engage a special teacher of these subjects. The choice of a good man was limited in those days, and Nicholas Rubinstein offered the post to Serov. Serov accepted, but immediately afterwards the success of his opera *Rogneda*, in St. Petersburg, made him unwilling to leave the modern capital for the less stirring atmosphere of Moscow. Rubinstein then resolved to engage the services of one of the first students who should qualify satisfactorily at the December examinations of the St. Petersburg

Conservatoire.   Kashkin, on hearing of this, showed Laroche's letter to Nicholas Rubinstein, and thus Tchaikovsky was marked out as a suitable applicant. Rubinstein, having subsequently interviewed the young composer in St. Petersburg, was so favourably impressed that he determined to appoint him to the post, disregarding even the advice of Zaremba, who recommended a more mature candidate.

Tchaikovsky entered upon his duties in Moscow early in January 1866.   The funds of the Musical Society were not then in a flourishing condition, and the expenses of the classes were kept as low as possible.   Tchaikovsky, as teacher of harmony, was to receive fifty roubles—about £6 : 5s.—per month until the opening of the Conservatoire.   He would have found some difficulty in living upon this extremely modest salary if Nicholas Rubinstein had not suggested to him to take up his quarters in his own flat, where he had already one inmate in the person of the violinist Shradik.   "In external appearance," says Kashkin, "Tchaikovsky produced a very favourable appearance, but the same cannot be said as to his dress.   He wore a very old fur pelisse which had been lent him by a friend, and the rest of his costume harmonised with this ancient *shuba*." Nicholas Rubinstein, who thought the young professor would be none the worse for a new frock-coat, was on the point of offering him credit at his own tailor's, when he remembered that Wieniawsky—who always stayed with him on his visits to Moscow—had, on the last occasion, left behind him a nearly new frock-coat.   It was fully a year since the virtuoso had departed, and, according to Russian custom, the coat belonged to the master of the house, who presented it, therefore, to Tchaikovsky.   It was a very bad fit, but Tchaikovsky did not trouble about that, and wore it, " with as much proud dignity as though it had been bought at the best tailor's in the town."

Kashkin was soon on terms of intimate friendship with his young colleague.   Tchaikovsky might easily have become as great a social favourite in Moscow as he had been in St. Petersburg, but he did not care much for society, and preferred to spend his evenings quietly with Kashkin, or his friend Jurgenson, the publisher.   He also frequented the Little Theatre, where the plays of Ostrovsky were the great attraction of the day.   An interesting feature of Moscow life at that time was the Artists' Club, founded by Nicholas Rubinstein, Ostrovsky, and Count Odoievsky.   Here the members often met to listen to the reading of some new literary work. Musical evenings were constantly organised, and every renowned virtuoso who passed through Moscow was certain to be heard at the Artists' Club.   Ladies were admitted, and dances held, at which the dance-music was provided by such artists as Nicholas Rubinstein and Wieniawsky.   At this club Tchaikovsky met Ostrovsky, one of the most celebrated writers of his day, who treated him with the greatest kindness, and afterwards generously provided him with the libretto of his first opera, *The Voievoda.* The earliest idols of Tchaikovsky's musical cult were

Glinka and Mozart, and he had a great veneration for the works of Beethoven. Schumann's fiery impulse and dreamy sentimentalism had a great attraction for him, and he inclined more to his music than to that of Chopin, in whom he found a note of invalidishness and a superfluity of subjective sentiment that somewhat repelled him. He greatly modified this opinion, however, after he had heard the works of Chopin interpreted by Nicholas Rubinstein. Tchaikovsky was well read in the literature of his own country, and his favourite authors were Ostrovsky and Tolstoi. He spoke French fluently, but of the German language and literature he knew very little in his younger days. Like most Russians, he was acquainted with Dickens and Thackeray through the medium of translations, but it was not until the last years of his life that he knew any English. Kashkin says that Tchaikovsky valued the morning hours for writing, and only under great pressure of work employed his evenings in composition. He would spend many hours reading music for four hands. His favourite relaxation was the game of *Yeralash* (a Russian form of whist). He was too absent-minded to become a good player, but bore the rebukes of irritable partners with the patient good-humour that seems always to have been his characteristic. "Tchaikovsky never defended himself when attacked, or began a quarrel," says Kashkin.

Tchaikovsky started his harmony class upon the system of his master Zaremba. Afterwards he became more independent in his methods, and laid great stress on the value of thorough-bass ; half his harmony course consisted of exercises in this subject. He never considered himself a good teacher, and took up the work more from necessity than inclination. But his scrupulous accuracy, business - like habits, and wonderful memory for musical examples, made him a more valuable teacher than he himself believed. Shortly after his arrival in Moscow, Nicholas Rubinstein suggested to him to write something for performance at one of the concerts of the Musical Society. Rubinstein — who during two-thirds of the year taught for nearly nine hours a day —was very rarely at home, and saw next to nothing of the two young men who shared his rooms. They were not, however, very quiet quarters, for a series of pianoforte classes was held there, and this music, mingled with the strains of Shradik's fiddle, were very distracting to the young composer. He was driven to take refuge in a neighbouring inn which, though it was a favourite haunt of the University students, was generally deserted in the morning hours. In the comparatively peaceful atmosphere of "The Great Britain" Tchaikovsky worked out most of his earlier compositions. The new work —a *Concert Overture in C minor*—was duly finished and submitted to Rubinstein for approval.

The composer, however, was destined to meet with the first of a series of bitter disappointments. Nicholas Rubinstein was not favourably impressed by the work, and all idea of its performance came to an end.   Tchaikovsky was hurt by what seemed to him the captious quality of Rubinstein's criticisms, but he showed no resentment.   The time was too short to allow of his preparing another work, and the *Concert Overture in F major*, for small orchestra, written in St. Petersburg, took the place of the rejected composition.   Here again Rubinstein demurred, and insisted upon the overture being re-scored for full orchestra, a proceeding which, according to Laroche, quite spoilt its unity of character.   It was heard on 4th March 1866, at Rubinstein's benefit concert, and though it did not have an extraordinary success, it attracted the attention of musicians to its composer. " He was thirsting for support and encouragement," writes Kashkin, " but at that time he hardly found one or the other."   For the rest of the winter Tchaikovsky composed very little, but he planned the sketch of his first symphonic poem, *Winter Day Dreams* (*Zimnia Grozi*).

The next event of importance in his life was the opening of the Moscow Conservatoire in the autumn of 1866.   After an imposing ceremony, a banquet was given, at which the directors of the institution and the members of the teaching staff were present. Tchaikovsky, in spite of constitutional shyness, was a good speaker, and in an effective speech he proposed the prosperity of the sister Conservatoire of St. Petersburg.   The banquet was followed by music, and Tchaikovsky, who was resolved that the first music heard in the hall of the Conservatoire should be Glinka's, opened the impromptu concert by playing the Overture to *Russlan and Ludmilla* from memory. He would have been well received, if only from patriotic sentiments, but his technique and artistic feeling were of a quality to command attention in themselves. Nicholas Rubinstein now moved into rooms adjoining the Conservatoire, and Tchaikovsky went with him. A few months later they were joined by Laroche, who had been appointed to the Conservatoire. The presence of Laroche did much towards reconciling Tchaikovsky to life in Moscow ; for though, eventually, he grew very fond of the ancient town atmosphere, during the first years of his existence there he was always regretting St. Petersburg, with its modern and more progressive musical life.

During the autumn of 1866 he was chiefly occupied upon his symphonic poem, *Winter Day Dreams*. With regard to his method of work I will quote the words of his friend Kashkin :—
" Tchaikovsky has not infrequently been accused of excessive haste and negligence in his work. On what ground such an accusation is founded I do not know ; for, from the beginning to the end of his career, he finished his compositions with great care, and absolutely without haste. If his works were written in an unbroken series, this can be explained simply by his industry. Every day he spent some hours in composing, and the disinclination for work was unknown to him, at least in the morning. Unknown to him, too, was the usual Russian ' some day or other ' which has stolen time from so many of us.

Tchaikovsky had the immense advantage of superior discipline in his work. Perhaps he owed this to his first governess, a French lady, whose name I forget. She lived until recently in some little town in the south of France, and cherished the memory of her pupil. If I am not mistaken, he visited her a year, or less, before his death. When he told me of this visit he was evidently much touched. With all the vehemence and impressibility of his nature, Tchaikovsky was the personification of order and accuracy, especially in his work; and he always appreciated the value of time. When first he came to live in Moscow, although he was then six-and-twenty, he was still inexperienced and young in many things, especially in the material questions of life; but in all that concerned his work he was already mature, with a particularly elaborate method of work, in which all was foreseen with admirable judgment, and manipulated with the exactitude of the surgeon in operating. This knowledge saved him much time, and permitted him to work with what seemed to others an inconceivable rapidity."

As soon as the symphonic poem, *Winter Day Dreams*, was finished, Tchaikovsky started for St. Petersburg, to show the new work to his old masters, Zaremba and Anton Rubinstein. He still valued the musical appreciation of St. Petersburg far above that of Moscow, and it was his ambition to have the symphony produced at a concert of the Musical Society in that city. He was full of hope, and confident of approbation; but again disappointment

awaited him.   Rubinstein and Zaremba criticised the
work with unsparing severity, and decided that it
could not pass into the programme of the Musical
Society.   Zaremba objected chiefly to the second
theme of the first movement, and although this was
very satisfactory to the composer himself, he changed
it, and made many other alterations in deference to the
wish of his masters.   Even then the work did not
come up to their standard of excellence.   Finally, by
way of consolation, they agreed to give the two
middle movements, but they met with no success.
The symphony now exists in its original form,
except for the unfortunate second theme, of which
the composer could never again recall his first idea.
This disappointment had the effect of detaching
Tchaikovsky's sympathies from St. Petersburg.
Henceforward he grew more and more reconciled to
life in Moscow, and valued the appreciation he was
beginning to meet with there.

II

In the winter of 1866-67 Tchaikovsky was engaged upon his first opera, *The Voievoda*. During a summer holiday to Hapsaal, on the coast of the Baltic, he wrote the pianoforte pieces *Souvenir de Hapsaal* (op. 2), of which No. 3, *Chant sans paroles*, has become such a favourite. By the autumn of 1867 a considerable portion of *The Voievoda* was written, including the orchestral number, "Dances of the Serving Maids," which soon became very popular in Moscow. During that season Nicholas Rubinstein organised a concert in the Grand Theatre on behalf of the sufferers from the famine in Finland, and suggested that Tchaikovsky should conduct his own dances. This was his *début* as a conductor, and Kashkin describes the anxiety he felt on his friend's behalf. Just before the ordeal Kashkin went behind the scenes of the theatre to see how Tchaikovsky was feeling. He said that, to his great surprise, he did not feel in the least nervous, and Kashkin returned to his seat. But when the new conductor actually found himself face to face with the vast audience, all his courage ebbed away. He completely lost his head, and practically forgot to conduct at all. Fortunately the band were well acquainted with the "Dances," and thus a fiasco was averted. For twenty years after this experience Tchaikovsky never took up the baton again. But then, circumstances having obliged him to conduct a few performances of his opera *Cherevichek*, he conquered his nervousness to a great extent, and became very fond of conducting his own works. In the early spring of 1868 the symphony, *Winter Day Dreams* — rejected in St. Petersburg — met with so warm a reception in Moscow that the composer must have been partially consoled for its first failure.

Tchaikovsky, who was on good terms with the heads of the theatrical administration in Moscow, had not much difficulty in getting *The Voievoda* accepted for performance at the Grand Theatre. In this matter he also had the assistance of Nicholas Rubinstein, by far the most influential person in the musical world of Moscow. But the troubles of the unfortunate composer only began with the acceptance of his work. At that time Italian opera reigned triumphant in Russia, while Russian opera played the part of Cinderella to her more splendid sister. Old scenery, cast-off dresses, second-rate artists, were considered good enough for National Opera. Russian composers were not even permitted the advantage of the full orchestra, which was reserved exclusively for Italian nights; they had to put up with the small and inferior " ballet orchestra."

Merelli, the manager of the Italian company, rented the Grand Theatre about five nights a week, and was practically the master of the situation. At the rehearsals Tchaikovsky suffered a great deal. He was inexperienced, and does not seem to have distributed his parts judiciously, though the material at his command was, at the best, very unpromising.

Finocchi, who sang the part of the Voievoda, was a second-rate Italian singer, who had, moreover, the greatest difficulty in singing his part in the Russian language. Madame Menshikov, the soprano, who appeared as Maria Vasilievna, had a fine voice, but no discipline. The singers were not unwilling, but their capabilities, as musicians, were of a very poor order. For example, the whole of the final quartet of one act had to be cut out, because one voice part contained triplets as against two equal notes in another, and this proved an insuperable difficulty to the performers.

Tchaikovsky's shy and sensitive disposition made it extremely painful to him to criticise or find fault with the singers. At the rehearsals, too, he began to discover, too late for alteration, many of his own mistakes of inexperience. He was in despair, says Kashkin, and only longed for the ordeal to be over. Nicholas Rubinstein twice attended the rehearsals, and went away angry with the composer's apparently supine amiability, which was really only the expression of a fatalistic resignation. The first performance of

The Voievoda took place on 30th January 1869. It was given in all about ten times—not such a bad record for a national opera in those days. Kashkin, who has forgotten many of the details of the performance, thinks that the music, though not strong, was rather popular, and that the libretto, which was a kind of Italian opera travesty of Ostrovsky's fine work, was the poorest part of the work. Afterwards Tchaikovsky burnt the score, partly perhaps from a feeling of disappointment, though no doubt the fact of his having incorporated some of the music into a new opera, *The Oprichnik*, would account for this destruction of *The Voievoda*. Twenty years later Arensky wrote an opera, *A Dream on the Volga*, upon the same subject. This work Tchaikovsky admired very much, and valued more highly than his own immature effort.

The Voievoda was followed by a fantasia for orchestra, entitled *Destiny* (*Fatum*). Although the composer never revealed the fact, Kashkin thinks that some autobiographical interest attaches to this work. The following quotation from the poet Batioushkov served as a motto to "Destiny" :—

> Thou knowest what the white-haired Melchisedek
> Said when he left this life : Man is born a slave ;
> A slave he dies. Will even Death reveal to him
> Why thus he laboured in this vale of tears,
> Why thus he suffered, wept, endured—then vanished ?

These words were suggested to Tchaikovsky as an appropriate epigraph *after* the completion of the work, but the public took them as a sort of programme, and sought in the music for some definite connection with the words. The fantasia was performed on 15th March 1869, with some success. Tchaikovsky afterwards destroyed the score of *Destiny*, but as he was fully aware of the existence of all the orchestral parts, it may be presumed that a restoration of this work would not be altogether disrespectful to the wishes of the composer.

About this time he first made the acquaintance of Balakirev, the talented leader of the nationalist school. In 1867 Balakirev had succeeded Anton Rubinstein as conductor of the St. Petersburg Musical Society, and head of the Conservatoire. He took advantage of this position to forward the interests of the rising school of Russian composers, and among these he included Tchaikovsky. But these nationalist tendencies did not find favour with the committee of management, and he was compelled to resign both positions after a brief tenure of office. Tchaikovsky wrote a letter to the *Sovrimenie Lietopis*, protesting with great indignation against the injustice done to Balakirev, and this led to a friendship between the two musicians. In the spring of 1869 Balakirev moved from St. Petersburg to Moscow, and the relations grew still more intimate. To Balakirev's suggestion Tchaikovsky owed the plan of his *Romeo and Juliet* overture. " This is always associated in my mind," writes M. Kashkin, " with the memory of a lovely day in May, with verdant forests and tall fir trees, among which we three were taking a walk.   Balakirev understood, to a great extent, the nature of Tchaikovsky's genius, and knew that it was adequate to the subject he suggested. Evidently he himself was taken with the subject, for he explained all the details as vividly as though the work had been already written. The plan, adapted to sonato form, was as follows : First, an introduction of a religious character, representative of Friar Lawrence, followed by an *Allegro in B minor* (Balakirev suggested most of the tonalities), which was to depict the enmity between the Montagues and Capulets, the street brawl, etc. Then was to follow the love of Romeo and Juliet (second subject in D flat major), succeeded by the elaboration of both subjects. The so-called 'development'—that is to say, the putting together of the various themes in various forms—passes over to what is called, in technical language, the 'recapitulation'—in which the first theme, *Allegro*, appears in its original form, and the love-theme (D flat major) now appears in D major, the whole ending with the death of the lovers. Balakirev spoke with such conviction that he at once kindled the ardour of the young composer, to whom such a theme was extremely well suited." Tchaikovsky returned from his holiday in September with the overture practically finished. He had put his heart into the work, which seems to throb with youthful passion and tenderness. His friends were enthusiastic over its beauties, and prophesied a great success.   But an adverse fate seemed always to await the first performances of Tchaikovsky's works.

Romeo and Juliet was given at one of the concerts of the Musical Society on 4th March 1870. It chanced that just at that time a student of the Conservatoire, resenting a reprimand which had been administered by the director, Nicholas Rubinstein, brought an action against him, and, owing to the absence of any legal code applying to the institution, won a technical victory. Public opinion was all in favour of Rubinstein, and when, on the evening of 4th March, he appeared upon the platform to conduct the new overture, he was received with the most frantic demonstration, while Tchaikovsky's music was completely forgotten in the excitement. The *Romeo and Juliet* overture was afterwards published by Bote and Bock, of Berlin, in 1871, and underwent many changes before it attained its present curtailed form, as seen in a second edition of the same published in 1881. Somewhere about this time, Tchaikovsky received the plot of a fantastic opera, entitled *Mandragora*. The composer seems to have been much attracted to the subject, and only relinquished it with great regret when M. Kashkin had convinced him of its being quite unsuited for operatic treatment. Only one number of *Mandragora* was ever heard in public, the " Chorus of Insects," which was very popular, both in Moscow and St. Petersburg. It is highly melodious, and recalls in character Mendelssohn's music to *A Midsummer Night's Dream*.

Now that the announcement of some of Tchaikovsky's works is sufficient to draw a crowded and enthusiastic audience, it is pathetic to look back upon the constant series of disappointments which awaited him in his early days. Few composers have been more unlucky with their first works than this gentle and sensitive artist, possessed with an almost feminine craving for approval and encouragement. A certain hyper-sensitiveness to the criticism of his artistic schemes led to a characteristic reticence on the part of Tchaikovsky. Consequently few people ever heard of the creation and untimely end of his opera *Undine*. The idea was probably suggested by the ready-made libretto which Count Sollogoub had written for A. Th. Lvov as early as 1848, and which was republished in Smirdin's edition of this author's works. The opera was finished early in 1870, and sent to St. Petersburg for the approval of the Theatrical Direction. Once he had completed and posted the score, and thus practically burnt his boats, Tchaikovsky spoke of the opera to a few intimate friends and played them some numbers from the work. *Undine* was rejected unconditionally, and the score, mislaid by the carelessness of some official, whom Tchaikovsky was too good-natured to expose, was not returned to him until some years later, when he destroyed it. One air, "Undine's Song," afterwards appeared as Lel's air in his music to Ostrovsky's "Snow Maiden." He took the rejection of his opera more philosophically than might be expected; but his mind was already occupied with a new scheme—the opera which afterwards appeared as *The Oprichnik*.

"Tchaikovsky," says Kashkin, "did not devote himself to the serious study of music until comparatively late; consequently he had not those definite and settled views upon music which seem a part of those who have grown up from childhood in a musical environment and have imbibed certain ideas and sympathies with life itself. He was obliged to acquire all this by means of hard work and the study of musical literature. As far as I can remember at that period (1870), he did not read orchestral scores with great ease, and preferred to make acquaintance with symphonic literature by the help of pianoforte arrangements for four hands, when I was often his partner at the piano. Of chamber music—especially string quartets—he knew very little at that time, and even the very character of this kind of music he appreciated with difficulty. The mere quality and *timbre* of the string quartet provoked in him nothing but weariness in those days, and he could hardly endure Beethoven's later quartets. He confessed to me once that he could scarcely keep awake in his seat through Beethoven's great A minor quartet. As to the combination of piano and stringed instruments, he admired many works of this class, especially those of Beethoven; but said he could not imagine himself writing for such a combination of instruments." Before long, however, he greatly modified his opinion, and even set to work upon this particular form of composition. Tchaikovsky was very anxious to spend the summer of 1871 abroad, but had no funds at his disposal. At the suggestion of Nicholas Rubinstein, he resolved to give a concert for his own benefit and produce some new work. As everything had to be organised on a modest and economical scale, there was no possibility of engaging an orchestra, and Tchaikovsky was driven to write his first string quartet in D. The *Andante* of this work has an interesting history, showing how Tchaikovsky valued national airs, and the cleverness with which he made use of them on occasion.

For several mornings the composer was awakened by the singing of a plasterer working upon the house just below his window. The workman's song haunted Tchaikovsky, who wrote down the air, and afterwards, at dinner-time, he sought out the singer and asked him to sing the words. They proved uninteresting, indeed almost devoid of meaning, as is so often the case with the townsfolk's version of the peasant's songs. The melody in its original form appears as No. 14 in Rimsky-Korsakov's collection of " A Hundred National Russian Songs."

Tchaikovsky's first concert, though not a colossal success, realised a sufficient sum to allow of his carrying out his trip abroad. Among the audience was the great novelist Turgeniev, who seems to have been impressed by Tchaikovsky's genius.

In 1870, Tchaikovsky's circumstances having considerably improved, he moved—greatly to the regret of Nicholas Rubinstein—into lodgings of his own. His way of life, even then, was by no means luxurious. He kept but one servant, a young country fellow, whose culinary skill never advanced beyond an unvarying daily dish of cabbage-soup and groats. But the composer was not fastidious, and in his new home he found the absolute quiet so indispensable for his creative work.

"About this time," writes M. Kashkin, "Tchaikovsky greatly admired a lady who sang in the Italian Opera Company. He was attracted by her talent as a singer, her ready wit, and brilliant conversational powers. His friends believed that he had fallen in love with this fascinating artist, and rumour had already decided their future, when the opera company left Moscow for Warsaw. During their visit to the Polish capital a telegram arrived, announcing the unexpected news of her marriage to another member of the company. Tchaikovsky seemed more astonished than hurt; but when, during the following season, the lady reappeared in Moscow, he was moved—even to tears—at the first sight of her upon the stage. Seven or eight years later I was present at an unexpected meeting between Tchaikovsky and this singer. He had gone to call upon Nicholas Rubinstein at the Conservatoire, but, on being told that he was engaged with a lady in his private room, we sat down in the ante-room to wait until the visitor should take her departure. Presently the door opened and the lady appeared. Tchaikovsky recognised her at a glance and sprang from his seat, turning very pale. The lady gave a little cry of alarm, and in her confusion began to fumble for the door of the half-lighted ante-room.

Having found it, she fled without a word. Nicholas Rubinstein, who had followed her out, stood a silent and astonished spectator of this little scene." A year or two later Tchaikovsky met the lady once more, while travelling abroad, and resumed his friendly relations with her. He still admired her gifted and charming disposition, but his passion—if it ever existed, save in his own imagination—had quite worn itself out. At any rate, he assured M. Kashkin, his feelings at that time were purely platonic.

About the same time that he was engaged upon the opera *Undine*, Tchaikovsky wrote his first songs: Six Songs (op. 6). These songs, though by no means the best that Tchaikovsky has written, are sufficiently characteristic to foreshadow most of his virtues and defects as a song-writer. There is no denying the extraordinary charm, the penetrating sweetness and melancholy, the vocal excellence of many of Tchaikovsky's songs. At the same time, if we compare him in this respect with Schubert and Schumann, with Brahms and Franz, or with his fellow-countrymen Dargomijsky and Balakirev, it is impossible to regard him as one of the greatest among song-writers. Nearly all his songs would be condemned if tried by the standard of formal perfection. His greatest weakness as a song-writer lies in the fact that he never realised the principle that, in the ideal song, music and poetry must meet upon an equal footing. " The union of the two arts," says Cui, " appeared to Tchaikovsky in the light of a *més-*

alliance for the one which he represented." Starting with this idea, that music is the only element of real importance in song, Tchaikovsky does not hesitate to mutilate the text of the greatest poets, to interpolate such exclamations as "good heavens," "alas," "woe is me," and occasionally by a stroke of his arbitrary pen to turn fine verse into indifferent prose. Perhaps it was on account of his contempt for poetry as the "worser half" of music that he has set comparatively few words by the great Russian poets, and prefers the effusions of such poetasters as Grekov and Sourikov. A fault which is common in Tchaikovsky's orchestral music is also noticeable in his songs. Not always very fastidious in his choice of musical ideas, he seems to find a difficulty in quitting them. He will develop, vary, and repeat an idea with a kind of mechanical skilfulness which becomes wearisome. He had not the qualities of terseness and concentration which go to the making of a perfect song. Another fault—though many may consider it an added fascination—in Tchaikovsky's songs is the monotonous vein of sentimental melancholy. The great preponderance of the "tearful minor" in his songs suggests an unhealthy condition of mind. And I would point out this difference between Tchaikovsky's melancholy and that of his fellow-countrymen, of whom we may take Moussorgsky as a characteristic type : that in the first instance it is subjective, and sometimes artificial; while in the second it is objective and called into being by the sufferings of others. It is just the

difference between "la belle mélancholie," so assid-
uously cultivated by Lamartine and his contemporaries, and "la tristesse de la vérité," which shows
so grimly in modern realism.   But although these
depreciative remarks apply to a large proportion
of Tchaikovsky's songs, especially his early ones,
there are a few which show the master-hand, many
potentially fine songs in spite of their want of form,
and many, again, which we would not have otherwise
than they are — songs we cannot criticise when
we hear them, because they take our feelings by
storm.

In 1871 the Society of the Friends of National
Science celebrated the bicentenary of the birth of
Peter the Great by what was called the Polytechnic
Exhibition.   For the opening ceremony Tchaikovsky
was commissioned to write a cantata to an appropriate
libretto by the poet Polonsky.   The work was heard
once, and then — with the exception of some material
introduced later on into the *Third Symphony* — all
trace of it wholly disappeared.   Tchaikovsky during
the next year or two was so deeply engaged upon his
new works, especially *The Oprichnik*, that he completely forgot this composition and took no steps to
save it from oblivion.   During the following year
(1872) Tchaikovsky published his *Harmony Primer*,
which has been adopted as one of the text-books at
the Moscow Conservatoire.

During the rebuilding of the Little Theatre in
1873, all the companies — dramatic, operatic, and
ballet — were obliged to take refuge on the boards

of the Great Theatre.   Under these conditions it
occurred to M. Begichev, the inspector of the theatrical repertory, to utilise the services of the entire
force in a kind of fairy play.   Ostrovsky undertook
the libretto, and chose for his subject the legend of
the "Snow Queen"—*Snegourotchka* ; while the music
was entrusted to Tchaikovsky.   Both the author and
the musician took immense pleasure in their task.
The sudden waking of the Russian spring never failed
to stir Tchaikovsky, and this season always found
him in his most exalted poetical mood.   The composition of the music to this legend of springtide
coincided with the coming of spring itself.   In little
more than three weeks the score was completed, in
spite of the fact that Tchaikovsky was working
twenty-seven hours a week at the Conservatoire.
The first performance of *The Snow Queen* took place
on 11th May 1873, but although its interpretation
was undertaken by the best artists, and no expense
spared in the mounting of the piece, it was not a
success.   The lack of dramatic interest outweighed
the charm of the music.   Shortly after the production
of *The Snow Queen*, Tchaikovsky, with M. Kashkin,
Nicholas Rubinstein, and one or two of the leading
artists taking part in the piece, made an excursion to
Vorobiev's Hill, a favourite resort in the neighbourhood of Moscow.   "It was a lovely spring day,"
writes the author of the *Reminiscences*, "and the
gardens of the village of Vorobiev were white with
a sheet of blossom.   Under the influence of spring
and *The Snow Queen*, we were all in a very happy

mood. The peasants soon gathered round to watch
'the quality' take their meal *al fresco* on the grass,
and Nicholas Rubinstein arranged a real rustic feast,
having bought for the peasants such sweets and wine
as he could find in the village shops. Nicholas
Rubinstein was very fond of genuine folk-music, and
invited the peasants to sing. They needed no pressing, and soon started their choral dances. This
scene must have always remained in Tchaikovsky's
mind, and it was resuscitated years later, when he
wrote the variations in the Pianoforte Trio, dedicated
to the memory of 'a great artist'—Nicholas Rubinstein."

The Snow Queen consists of an Introduction
to the play, of several entr'actes and dances, and
includes a few choruses and solo numbers. The
music is fresh and melodious, though not always
of a high quality. The Introduction and the
second entr'acte are the most successful parts of
the work. Berezovsky considers that in some
parts *The Snow Queen* shows that Tchaikovsky
was very much influenced by Schumann at the time.
Rimsky-Korsakov has also written a fairy opera to
Ostrovsky's text, which, as regards imaginative
treatment and national colouring, is superior to
Tchaikovsky's work.

Some time during the early spring of 1874,
Tchaikovsky finished his *Second Quartet in F major*,
and it was privately performed at Nicholas Rubinstein's rooms in the presence of his more illustrious
brother Anton. This occasion may serve as an

example of the inexplicable attitude of Anton Rubinstein towards the compositions of his former pupil. "I know," writes M. Kashkin, "that Rubinstein was very fond of Tchaikovsky as a man, and valued his talent very highly, but at the same time he took an almost hostile view of the majority of his compositions, especially the great ones. As a pianist he almost ignored Tchaikovsky's works. . . . The *Quartet in F major* was played before a very small audience ; besides the players Laut, Grijimal, Fitzenhagen, and Herber—who, I believe, played second violin—there were present only Albrecht, Hubert, Anton Rubinstein, and myself. All the time the music went on, Rubinstein listened with a lowering, discontented expression, and at the end, with his usual brutal frankness, he said that it was not in the least in the style of chamber music ; that he himself could not understand the composition, etc. The audience as well as the players went into ecstasies ; but the one listener whose appreciation meant most to the composer obstinately stuck to his own opinion. One word from him would have been more valued than all other praise or success, but Tchaikovsky was not destined to hear that word, and he was evidently deeply hurt by Rubinstein's cutting remarks. It did not, however, shake his devotion to his former master. When, about a year later, he dedicated one of his piano pieces to Tchaikovsky, the latter was delighted, and replied by dedicating to Anton Rubinstein his *Six Pieces on one Theme* (op. 21) ; but he received no acknowledgment, and the great virtuoso never played one of these pieces in public."

From 1872 to 1876 Tchaikovsky acted as musical critic to the *Sovremennaya Lietopis* and the *Russky Vestnik*.

III

In 1872 the Conservatoires of Moscow and St. Petersburg had the misfortune to lose their most influential patroness, the Grand Duchess Helena Paulovna. Shortly before her death she had requested her favourite composer, Serov, to write an opera upon the subject of Gogol's " Christmas Eve Revels," for which Polonsky prepared the libretto. But Serov, who was just then engaged upon his opera *The Power of Evil*, had only time to complete one number of the new work when death put an end to his labours, and he breathed his last only an hour later than his patroness the Grand Duchess. Out of respect to the memory of this remarkable woman, the directors of the Imperial Musical Society resolved to carry out her wishes respecting this opera, and a competition was organised for the best setting of *Vakoula the Smith* (*Kouznetz Vakoula*), as Polonsky's libretto was entitled.

Tchaikovsky had not hitherto been very successful in his operatic works, and he hesitated for some time to take part in this competition. Consequently, when at last he decided to do so, he was obliged to work very rapidly in order to finish the opera by August 1874. Seven works were sent in for approval, and both the first and second prizes were awarded to Tchaikovsky's composition. All his friends were interested in the new work, and, encouraged by his success, Tchaikovsky, contrary to custom, volunteered to play through the whole score to a select audience of intimate friends. He was too nervous, however, to do justice to the work. "The performer killed the composer," and the opera, rendered in a pointless and spiritless fashion, produced an unfavourable impression which the audience could scarcely disguise. Afterwards, when the printed score appeared, his friends recognised with astonishment that *Kouznetz Vakoula* was one of Tchaikovsky's strongest dramatic efforts. The work was first performed at the Marinsky Theatre, St. Petersburg, in November 1876. It was sumptuously mounted, and the parts entrusted to picked artists. Even the small rôle of the *Golova* (headman of the village) was taken by Petrov, the renowned *doyen* of the Russian stage. *Kouznetz Vakoula* was received with enthusiasm, but its success was ephemeral. The public had expected a light comic opera in the French style, and did not appreciate the national element in Tchaikovsky's music. It was given about seventeen times, and then disappeared from the repertory. The composer himself considered this opera one of his best works. Later on he remodelled it under the title of *Cherevichek* ("The little Shoes").

The year 1873 saw the production of two important orchestral compositions : the *Second Symphony in C minor*, and the orchestral fantasia on the subject of Shakespeare's *Tempest*. Tchaikovsky's *Second Symphony*, which was written a year or two before the opera *Vakoula the Smith*, is one of the most interesting examples of purely Russian symphonic music, and has been aptly called the Little-Russian Symphony, because its first and last movements are based on Malo-Russian melodies. It may here be noted that the difference between the folk-music of the Great Russians and the Malo-Russians is as great as the difference in character between the two races ; consequently this symphony has a peculiar character of its own to which it owes its title, and not—as one critic has sapiently observed—to the fact that it is based on *small* Russian themes. The *Second Symphony* is perhaps the most distinctively national of all Tchaikovsky's works. The first *Allegro* is preceded by an Introduction founded on a beautiful melody of an elegiac character which runs straight into the *Allegro*. The first subject of this movement is a variant of the well-known air, "Down by Mother Volga." This is one of the songs associated with the Cossack robber Stenka Razin, whose "rebellious head"—as the ballad has it—was cut off in the Red Square, at Moscow, in 1671, and it is a great favourite among Russian students. The second movement, *Andantino marciale*, has one very interesting subject which the composer borrowed from the march in *Undine*, the unpublished opera of which he had destroyed the score. The *Finale*, which is generally considered the best movement of the symphony, has two remarkable themes treated in variation form. The first of these is taken from the Little-Russian song called " The Crane " ; the second —a beautiful melody—is original. The symphony is full of vitality, movement, and racy humour, and, according to Berezovsky, it shows in sentiment and workmanship a strong reflection of Glinka's influence. It was first performed in Moscow at a concert of the Russian Musical Society in 1873, and was received with great applause, but Tchaikovsky, who was easily discouraged when his own work was in question, was persuaded by some hypercritical friends to make great changes in the symphony before it was published. " I always preferred the original form," says Kashkin, " and fortunately it might be restored, at least for purposes of comparison, for the orchestral parts used at the first performance are still preserved in the library of the Moscow Conservatoire."

A work of a totally different character was the symphonic fantasia *The Tempest*, composed during a month's holiday at a country house in the government of Tambov. It was written to a programme suggested by M. Vladimir Stassov, who has so often inspired the composers for the New Russian school with subjects for musical illustration. M. Stassov in one of his letters has given me the following account of its origin :—

" In 1872 I was very intimate with Tchaikovsky, and in constant correspondence with him. As he

had observed with pleasure the various subjects for
overtures, operas, and symphonies which I had
recently suggested to some of my friends among the
Russian composers, he asked me to find him a suitable subject for an overture. At first I refused,
saying that for each individual composer one must
only choose a theme completely in keeping with his
nature and temperament, and that I did not feel that
I knew his tastes and disposition well enough to
undertake the task. However, he would not accept
my refusal, and wrote me several letters, pressing me
to yield, and saying that *no one was more capable than
myself of finding a subject which would fascinate him.*
I then gave in, and having tried him with several
subjects—beginning with Scott's "Kenilworth," which
did not please him much—I finally proposed Shakespeare's *Tempest*, a subject I had been mad about ever
since my young days. Tchaikovsky was delighted,
and wrote me back a warm reply, saying nothing
could have suited him better, that he was full of
enthusiasm, and could think of nothing else. He
accepted my programme in all its details, without the
least change, and the work, he said, must and should
be dedicated to no one but myself. Shortly afterwards all this was faithfully carried out."

Stassov's programme stands as follows : " The sea.
Ariel, spirit of the air, raises a tempest in obedience
to the will of the enchanter Prospero. Wreck of
the vessel conveying Ferdinand. The enchanted
island. The first shy awakening of love between
Miranda and Ferdinand. Ariel. Caliban. The

enamoured pair give themselves up to the magic of love. Prospero divests himself of his powers of enchantment and quits the island. The sea." The subjects are fresh and poetical. The picture of the sea, both in storm and in undulating calm, is highly effective ; especially the chords for trombones in the lower register, which give a wonderful sense of strength and repose. The Ariel theme is very sprightly, and treated with appropriate lightness and grace. It is followed by a bold, rough figure, given out by celli and basses, which effectively symbolises the uncouth Caliban. Prospero's *Leitmotif*, which has almost a religious character, seems the least appropriate of all these characteristic themes. The most noticeable fault of the fantasia is one common to most of Tchaikovsky's works, namely the irritating repetition of certain phrases which finally wearies the nerves of the hearer and ends in a temporary suspension of interest. *The Tempest* was performed at the Paris Exhibition in 1873, and was enthusiastically received.

To this period belongs the *Pianoforte Concerto in B flat minor* (op. 25). M. Kashkin gives an interesting account of the birth of this work. He writes :—

"Tchaikovsky, who had long had it in his mind to compose a pianoforte concerto for Nicholas Rubinstein, set about this work in the winter of 1874. The task proved a difficult one, because the invention of passages for the piano combined with orchestra did not come easily to him ; but he did not shrink from difficulties, and in February 1875 the composition was quite ready. Tchaikovsky took the finished score to Nicholas Rubinstein, and on the title-page was inscribed the dedication to him. Tchaikovsky himself was very well satisfied with his composition, upon which he had worked hard and with zeal. The composer looked forward to the fullest approval, more especially as his friend and adviser always evinced the warmest interest in his compositions and his talent generally. This time it turned out very differently. Nicholas Rubinstein, it appeared, was disagreeably surprised that Tchaikovsky —not being a pianist—had not asked his advice about the piano part, and therefore he showed prejudice and hostility as regards this work. At the trial of the concerto N. A. Hubert and myself were the only auditors. Nicholas Rubinstein, who read admirably at sight, started the concerto, and began finding fault with everything, but especially with the piano technique. He played even with a certain intentional clumsiness, finding it all unsuitably written, too difficult, and finally declaring it altogether unplayable from this point of view, and in need of great alteration. N. A. Hubert did not pronounce a definite judgment, but seemed to agree with Rubinstein; while Tchaikovsky was burning with anger against them both. Generally speaking, he had so great a respect for Nicholas Rubinstein as a pianist and musician that no doubt he would have agreed with him as to all the alterations if his criticisms had been made in a more conciliatory spirit; but so harsh a judgment merely irritated him, and he resolved to publish the concerto without altering a single note; only the original dedication was struck out and replaced by one to Hans von Bülow, whose acquaintance Tchaikovsky had made during the previous year. Von Bülow was delighted with the concerto, as I saw from a letter of his to Tchaikovsky, which was shown to me ; and as he was just starting on a long concert tour in America, he included in his programme the work which had been dedicated to him. Thus it happened that Tchaikovsky's *B flat minor Concerto* was heard for the first time in Boston, U.S.A. Bülow sent Tchaikovsky a telegram announcing the brilliant success of his work. Of course this news gratified the composer ; but just then he happened to be very short of money, and it was not without some compunction that he spent it all in answering the message. In Moscow the concerto was played for the first time by S. J. Taneiev, with great success; and afterwards Nicholas Rubinstein actually learnt it, and his playing of it was such as one could hardly hear from any other artist. He had a particular success with it at the Russian concerts at the Paris Exhibition of 1878." Speaking of this work, Mr. C. A. Barry says : " That N. Rubinstein was not altogether over-severe in his strictures of Tchaikovsky's piano technique, appears from the fact that at a subsequent date Tchaikovsky thoroughly overhauled his work, and issued a new and revised edition of it in 1889, when it was found that the pianoforte part had, to a great extent, been rewritten."

IV

TCHAIKOVSKY worked with untiring perseverance, but the occupation of teaching grew more distasteful to him year by year. He dreamt of an ideal life in some quiet country place where he could give himself up entirely to composition. But he believed such an ideal existence to be, if not quite unattainable, at least very remote. The manner in which his dream was ultimately fulfilled reads like a fairy tale. In 1878 a lady, who preferred to keep her identity concealed, and who was not personally known to the composer, made it possible by her generous initiative for him to give up his classes at the Conservatoire and devote all his time to the creation of new works. Already in 1874 his improved means had permitted him to move from the small rooms in the Gudrinsky Place into a cosy flat, where he remained until his marriage in 1877.

In 1874 Tchaikovsky completed a new opera, *The Oprichnik*, in which he incorporated a good deal of musical material from *The Voievoda* and his symphonic poem *Destiny*. *The Oprichnik* is some-times translated by the somewhat misleading title of "The Lifeguardsman." The Oprichniks were a band of dissolute young noblemen, the chosen body-guard of Ivan the Terrible, who swore by fearful and unnatural oaths to carry out every command of the despot they served. Sometimes they masqueraded in the dress of monks, but they were in reality robbers and murderers, hated and feared by the people whom they oppressed. Andrew Morozov, the descendant of a noble but impoverished house, and the only son of the widowed Lady Morozova, is in love with the beautiful Natalia, daughter of Prince Jemchoujny. His poverty disqualifies him as a suitor. While desperately in need of money, Andrew falls in with Basmanov, a young Oprichnik, who persuades him to join the community, telling him that an Oprichnik can always fill his own pockets. Andrew consents, and takes the customary oath of celibacy. Afterwards circumstances cause him to break his vow and marry Natalia against her father's wish. Prince Viazminsky, the leader of the Oprichniks, cherishes an old grudge against the family of Morozov, and works for Andrew's downfall. On his wedding-day he breaks in upon the feast with a message from the Tsar. Ivan the Terrible has heard of the bride's beauty, and desires her attendance at the royal apartments. Andrew, with gloomy forebodings in his heart, prepares to escort his bride, when Viazminsky, with a meaning smile, explains that the invitation is for the bride *alone*. Andrew refuses to let his wife go into the tyrant's presence unprotected.   Viazminsky proclaims him a rebel and a traitor to his vows.   Natalia is carried away by force, and the Oprichniks lead Andrew into the market-place to suffer the death-penalty at their hands.   Meanwhile Lady Morozova, who had cast off her son when he became an Oprichnik, has softened towards him, and comes to seek him on his wedding-day.   She enters the deserted hall where Viazminsky, alone, is gloating over the success of his intrigue.   She inquires unsuspectingly for Andrew, and he leads her to the window. Horror-stricken, she witnesses the execution of her own son by his brother Oprichniks, and falls dead at the feet of her implacable enemy.

Tchaikovsky himself is answerable for the plot of the opera, and it would be difficult to find anything more tragic, even in the gloomy and blood-stained pages of mediæval Russian history; but it certainly offers great scope for dramatic development.

The opera opens with an overture in which all the leading motives and chief situations in the opera are more or less anticipated.   The curtain rises upon the garden of Prince Jemchoujny's house, where he is discovered in earnest conversation with Mitkov, his daughter's accepted suitor.   After they have left the stage, Natalia enters with her old nurse and a company of young girls, and there follows a charming chorus on a well-known Russian folk-song.   Then the girls beg Natalia for a song, and she complies with a pretty, plaintive melody, very vocal, but without any marked originality.   Next the Oprichniks come upon the scene, and their characteristic motive is heard in the orchestra. Basmanov meets Andrew Morozov, learns the secret of his depression, and offers to lend him some money, advising him at the same time to cast in his lot with theirs. The air "Come live among us," in which Basmanov seeks to entice the young man by promising him a life of adventure and full pockets in the future, seems quite inappropriate, being an elegant *cantilena* in the minor. After the solo, the orchestra has some bars illustrating the wild life of the Oprichniks. Andrew and Basmanov leave the garden together, and Natalia reappears, and, after a short recitative, sings a pretty air, "Ah, Furious Wind," quite Italian in character. The act ends with a second chorus of maidens, which makes an abrupt transition from the Italian to the national style.

The first scene of the second act takes place in the house of the Morozovs. The orchestra reflects the anxious forebodings with which Lady Morozova awaits her son's return. Then in an admirably characteristic recitative, which seems at once to distinguish her as the type of a high-minded religious woman, she expresses her faith in God and her resignation in all her misfortunes. Andrew now returns, and brings her the money Basmanov has given him. Lady Morozova refuses to touch what she knows to be the fruits of robbery and murder, and, in a long and touching scene, implores her son not to associate himself with the hated Oprichniks. Andrew, who is devoted to his mother, promises to obey her wishes. His solo in this act, "The White Snow," is one of the most successful, and at the same time national, numbers in the whole work.

The second scene takes us into the king's palace. It opens with a chorus (*à capella*) of the Oprichniks, who, attired as monks, are seen issuing from the royal oratory. At a sacrilegious word from their leader they throw aside their monastic garb and reveal their rich robes beneath. Basmanov introduces Andrew to the community, and he takes their vow. The first sacrifice demanded of him is the complete renunciation of his mother and Natalia. The music which depicts Andrew's inward struggle before he consents to give up all for the sake of retrieving his fortunes is often full of poignant dramatic feeling. The effect is enhanced by the gloomy chorus of the Oprichniks, which forms as it were the musical basis of the whole scene. Only, here again, Andrew's solo, with its occasional reminiscences of Rossini, seems out of keeping with the rest of the music.

The third act shows a square in Moscow. The townspeople are assembled, and in the opening chorus they bewail " that the times are evil." Then with an expression of almost fatalistic resignation and submissive piety, which is realistically characteristic of the Russian poor, they turn their lament into a touching and beautiful prayer : *Andante religioso*, " Thou, God, succour us." This scene is remarkably impressive. Lady Morozova now appears. She has suffered one more misfortune in the desertion of her son. She sings a pathetic recitative, " Now am I lonely." The children in the square catch sight of

Lady Morozova, and hail her with insulting epithets —"Mother of an Oprichnik," etc. But the older people are sorry for her afflictions, which are even greater than their own. She is about to enter the church, when Natalia hastens in. She has fled from her father and her middle-aged lover, and implores Lady Morozova to succour her. Her father now arrives, and orders his rebellious daughter to return home. Natalia's reply is given in an aria, "As before God, O father." Prince Jemchoujny will not relent, and orders his servants to carry off Natalia by force. His proceedings are interrupted by the arrival of the Oprichniks, awakening terror and hatred among the people. Andrew sees his mother and rushes to embrace her, while the sinister theme of the Oprichniks is heard reminding him of his vows. Lady Morozova turns from her son, disowns him, and solemnly curses him as an Oprichnik. The end of this scene is full of incident, and the music rises to a high level of dramatic interest.

The last act takes place in the king's palace. Andrew, unable to abandon Natalia to her fate, has determined to marry her in spite of his vows. The curtain draws up upon the wedding-feast, and some of the Oprichniks who are present sing a chorus in praise of the bride. The chorus is based upon a folk-song, and, though musically interesting, suffers from over-repetition. It is succeeded by national dances, for which also folk-songs are employed. The duet between Andrew and Natalia, "Ah, let the feast be ended soon," has two subjects, one of which

Tchaikovsky transferred from his unpublished symphonic poem *Destiny*. I have already described the tragic ending of the opera. The curtain falls to a chorus of the Oprichniks, heard off the stage as they return from the execution of Andrew : "Hail, hail ! Like the glorious sun at midday art thou, our father and our Tsar."

The Oprichnik, though by no means a faultless work, was a great advance on Tchaikovsky's earlier operas, *Undine* and *The Voievoda*. The chief shortcomings are a want of unity in the style of the music; a lack of decision in the portrayal of many of the characters—Lady Morozova is quite the most convincing and real of all the *dramatis personae*; an occasional want of connection between the music and the words, and perhaps, we must add, the unrelieved gloom of the libretto. In spite of all this the opera holds our attention. The music is always fluent, often very impressive, and, as might be expected from Tchaikovsky, it contains many beautiful melodies. It is not surprising, therefore, that *The Oprichnik* holds its own on the Russian stage. Its immediate success was sufficient to encourage Tchaikovsky to new efforts in the sphere of dramatic music.

In 1875 he wrote a work in the same tonality as his pianoforte concerto—the *Sérénade Mélancholique*, for violin and orchestra. It is based on two very interesting subjects : one of a melancholy nature, the other exceedingly passionate.

V

To the same year belongs his *Third Symphony in D* (op. 29), a work altogether different in style to his two earlier ones, and totally western in character. It has some emotional and intellectual affinity with the Schumann symphonies, but displays such brilliancy of orchestration as the German master never attained to. This symphony—which is exceedingly popular in Russia and abroad—has, in some mysterious way, acquired the title of "The Polish." The label is as misleading as unauthorised labels generally are. Certainly the symphony ends with an Allegro—*tempo di Polacca*, a very alien and artificial form of that genuine national dance, the polonaise ; but since the second movement is *alla tedesca*, would it not be just as reasonable—and from internal evidence far more appropriate—to christen the symphony "The German"? If there is not enough that is genuinely Polish in the musical material of the work to warrant the choice of this title, the idea that Tchaikovsky here poured out his sympathy for "Poland mourning

in her oppression and rejoicing in her regeneration"
is still more untenable. When we remember that
Tchaikovsky was exceedingly Russian in his sympathies, and that as the writer of *1812*, the *Marche
Slave*, and the *Triumphal Overture on the Danish
Hymn*, he may be regarded as the official composer
of Russia, it seems quite incredible. One would as
soon expect to find Mr. Rudyard Kipling writing an
ode in praise of the Little Englanders, or Mr. Kensit
a complimentary sonnet to the Pope. Berezovsky
gives the following brief account of this symphony :
" It consists of the customary four movements. The
first opens with a magnificent funeral march, which
leads to an allegro of a festal character, broadly
planned. The second begins with a graceful valse
alla tedesca, which afterwards gives place to an
Andante elegiaco. This *andante*, for its depth of
thought, its sincere and vital emotional qualities,
is the best movement of the whole symphony, and
one of the finest of musical conceptions. Here
Tchaikovsky's genius is displayed in all its force, in
all its varied character, and in the setting of his inimitable technique. In comparison with the *Andante*,
the third movement of the symphony—a *Scherzo*—
loses a great deal. Here expression predominates
over the contents, and leaves the impression of beautiful but uninspired music. The *Finale* is better than
the *Scherzo ;* it is written throughout in the major,
and the symphony ends as it were in dazzling sun-
shine. Performed in Paris in 1876, and in New
York in 1879, this work had great success, and

attracted the attention of Europe and America to its composer."

The year 1875 also saw the publication of four sets of songs, op. 16, 25, 27, and 28. The first set, op. 16, contains two of Tchaikovsky's best : the graceful "Slumber Song," and "A Modern Greek Song," founded on a *Dies Irae* of the Middle Ages, and treated with consummate skill. In op. 25 are "Reconciliation" and "Mignon's Song." Op. 27 contains, among others, two songs in mazurka form to words by Miczkievich, which are not very well known in England. Op. 28 is a very remarkable collection, containing "The Coral Necklace," one of his most dramatic songs; "Wherefore"; the charming and characteristic "He loves me well"; and "The Dread Moment," an expression of wild, despairing passion.

In March 1875 Tchaikovsky's nerves broke down, and the doctors ordered him abroad, forbidding him to touch the piano or a sheet of music-paper. He followed these orders more strictly in the letter than in the spirit. Perhaps it would have been impossible to check entirely the creative activity of his mind ; in any case, he returned with a new composition complete in his brain, though not a note had been committed to paper. The violinist Laub died in the spring of 1875, and Tchaikovsky, who had the warmest admiration for his talent, honoured his memory by the *E flat Quartet*. The date upon the MS. of this quartet (in the possession of P. Jurgenson) is February 1876, but M. Kashkin seems to have no doubt as to its having been composed a year earlier. At this time the editor of the *Nouvelist*—a St. Petersburg magazine—commissioned Tchaikovsky to write twelve short pieces, to appear monthly, under the general title of *The Seasons*. An amusing anecdote is told in connection with these pieces. Tchaikovsky, who was afraid of forgetting this little commission, told his servant—who was devoted to him—to remind him when the date came round for sending off a piece. The man never forgot, and every month he used to say to his master, "Peter Ilich, this is your day for sending to Petersburg." Tchaikovsky would go to his desk, dash off the composition, and dispatch it by the next post.

Opera was the species of composition that offered the greatest attraction to Tchaikovsky, and after that some orchestral work on a large scale, though now and then he would publish a series of songs, or " romances," as the Russians call them. Like most of his fellow-countrymen, he was, at that period of his life, a devotee of the ballet, and had long cherished the idea of producing something of this kind. The opportunity came at last when Begichev, stage-manager of the Grand Theatre at Moscow, proposed to Tchaikovsky to write a ballet. The latter agreed, but stipulated for a fantastic subject from the Age of Chivalry, and Begichev himself sketched out the plot for *The Swan Lake*, for which Tchaikovsky consented to supply the music for 800 roubles— about £100. His ideal ballet in those days was

Giselle, the joint production of Theóphile Gautier and Adolphe Adam. The ballet was begun and finished in the summer of 1876, and the pianoforte score was arranged by M. Kashkin. At the request of the ballet-master, a national dance—quite out of keeping with the rest—was added to the work. The success of *The Swan Lake*, if not brilliant, was fairly lasting. It continued to be given until the scenery and dresses became shabby, when the authorities did not take any steps to restore the *mise en scène*. The music, too, underwent a great many changes, being gradually replaced by airs from other ballets until only about a third of the original was left. Recently *The Swan Lake* has been very successfully revived in St. Petersburg.

Two pieces of a more or less occasional character were produced in the course of 1876. The *Triumphal Overture on the Danish National Hymn*, was written for the visit of the Princess Dagmar to Moscow, and is on the whole superior to the general run of such works. A more interesting and inspired creation is the *Marche Slave*. The war between Turkey and Servia, in 1876, was the occasion of a great display of Slavonic enthusiasm. Nicholas Rubinstein organised a concert for the benefit of the wounded, for which Tchaikovsky, who was in full sympathy with the feelings of the hour, composed a march, first known as the " Russo-Servian," but afterwards as the "Slavonic March." It had a great success, being a stirring presentment of the emotions which just then were dominant in Russia, and in some measure it was prophetic of the triumph of the Slavonic cause.

Another great work belonging to this period is the third orchestral fantasia *Francesca di Rimini*, which was originally conceived as an opera. The libretto was brought to Tchaikovsky by the author, K. I. Zvantsev, and the composer, who was well satisfied with it, was about to begin the work, when the librettist attempted to impose some impossible conditions. Zvantsev was an almost fanatical Wagnerite, and insisted that his book should be treated according to Wagnerian principles; but the Russian composer refused to relinquish his complete liberty of action, and the opera was consequently abandoned. His imagination, however, had been fired by the subject, and he could not refrain from using up his ideas in some different form. Tchaikovsky informed M. Kashkin that Doré's drawings for Dante's "Divine Comedy" had had a considerable influence upon his picture of "Hell's Whirlwind." If so, the painter's conception gained immensely in impressiveness and dignity by its reincarnation in the musician's mind. Tchaikovsky's realism is of a far more poetic quality than Doré's, and singularly free, in this instance, from mere sensationalism. Tchaikovsky prefaces his score with the following passages from Dante's "Inferno," Canto V. (Cary's translation) :—

"Dante, coming into the second circle of Hell, witnesses the punishment of carnal sinners, who are tossed about ceaselessly in the dark air by the most furious winds. Amongst these, he

meets with Francesca of Rimini, who relates her
story :—

> . . . No greater grief than to remember days
> Of joy, when misery is at hand.   That kens
> Thy learn'd instructor.   Yet so eagerly
> If thou art bent to know the primal root,
> From whence our love gat being, I will do
> As one who weeps and tells his tale.   One day,
> For our delight we read of Lancelot,
> How him love thrall'd.   Alone we were, and no
> Suspicion near us.   Oft-times by that reading
> Our eyes were drawn together, and the hue
> Fled from our alter'd cheek.   But at one point
> Alone we fell.   When of that smile we read,
> The wished-for smile so rapturously kissed
> By one so deep in love, then he, who ne'er
> From me shall separate, at once my lips
> All trembling kiss'd.   The book and writer both
> Were love's purveyors.   In its leaves that day
> We read no more.   Thus while one spirit spake,
> The other wailed so sorely, that heart-struck
> I, through compassion fainting, seem'd not far
> From death, and like a corse fell to the ground.

The two first movements of the fantasia —
Andante lugubre and *Piu mosso*—are clearly intended
to illustrate the prose passages from the Argument.
To the *Allegro vivo* which succeeds it is difficult to
assign a definite connection with the text ; but with
the clarinet cadenza at the close of this movement,
and the lovely melody which follows it—a melody
so entirely characteristic of Tchaikovsky's genius—
we seem to hear the spirit-voice of Francesca herself,
from which all the horrors of Hell have not taken the
sweetness of human love and poignant memory.

Immediately after the completion of *Francesca di Rimini*, he made a rough sketch of his *Fourth Symphony in F minor*. But already a new conception possessed him, which for the time being drove all others from his mind—this was the idea of *Eugene Oniegin*.

VI

In May 1877, during the examinations at the Conservatoire, Tchaikovsky first confided to M. Kashkin his intention of writing an opera on the subject of Poushkin's celebrated "novel in verse," *Eugene Oniegin*. For the germ of this idea he was indebted to the celebrated Russian singer, Elizabeth Andrecona Lovrovsky. For several evenings in succession M. Kashkin and Tchaikovsky sat up half the night, in a private room of Taistov's Restaurant, trying to sketch out a feasible plot that should not depart too much from Poushkin's poem. The task proved almost beyond their powers, and finally Tchaikovsky declared that though he despaired of adapting *Eugene Oniegin* for operatic purposes, he still felt impelled to write something on the subject, in order to use up the many ideas which had taken root in his mind. Feeling that his work might not be suitable for a big stage, he persuaded Nicholas Rubinstein to let it be performed by the pupils of the Conservatoire, and, happy in this assurance, he threw himself heart and soul into the new project, after securing the services of Shilovsky as collaborator in the libretto.

Probably no one was more astonished than Tchaikovsky himself when he found that this work, from which he expected very little beyond personal satisfaction and a pretty operatic performance for the Conservatoire students, was destined to prove not only his most successful work, but—if we except Glinka's *Life for the Tsar*—the most popular opera in all Russia. The secret of this success lies partly in the subject itself, which is known to every reading man and woman in the land; partly in the very melodious and accessible character of the music; and partly, again, in the fact that in *Eugene Oniegin* Tchaikovsky had hit upon a subject which, though it did not call forth the very greatest that was in him, was, on the whole, pre-eminently suited to his genius, and especially to his melancholy lyricism. But though the opera is by far the most successful of Tchaikovsky's works, and in respect of popularity would soon become a rival to "The Pathetic" Symphony and *Casse-Noisette Suite*, it is by no means his best. There are really great moments in *The Oprichnik*; in *Eugene Oniegin* there are moments of extraordinary weakness and banality. But the former will interest the educated minority in spite of its faults; while the latter will take "the great public" by storm, and be loved for these very weaknesses themselves. There is a great affinity—in certain moods— between the genius of Poushkin and that of Tchaikovsky. Both had at times the gift of wearing their hearts on their sleeves in a very graceful, and not too unmanly, fashion. It is the gift of all others that has most attraction for the great public, who resent nothing so much as the failure to read the man in his work. The sentimentality, the false pathos, the Byronic cynicism of *Eugene Oniegin*, would have been far less attractive but for the thinly-veiled auto-biographic interest of the story. As it is, probably every Russian youth has fancied himself an Oniegin or a Lensky; every Russian girl has played at being Tatiana. And Tchaikovsky has attuned himself without difficulty to the subjective and sentimental mood of the poet, which was so often his own most characteristic temper of mind — though not his highest. The result in both cases is a work of almost unparalleled popularity.

The characters in the story offer several strongly-marked contrasts, of which Tchaikovsky has not availed himself in his musical presentment of them. The sisters, Tatiana and Olga, are two very different types of Russian girlhood. Tatiana is dreamy, sentimental, naïve, without coquetry; capable of folly for love's sake, but incapable of dishonour. Olga— as she appears in the book of the opera—is full of animal spirits, practical, and a reckless flirt. The girls belong to any period. The young men, on the contrary, seem essentially "dated." Lensky, the sensitive, morbid, passionate youth, fresh from a German university, belongs to the Byronic period. So, too, does Oniegin, the cold-blooded, cultured, world-weary young rake, who works such havoc in the quiet home of the Lerins.

The opera opens with an Introduction founded on the dreamy, graceful subject which is Tatiana's *Leitmotif*. Later on we hear the subject of the duet between Tatiana and Oniegin, and then the music reverts to the first theme. " Thus," says Berezovsky, " the essence of the drama is revealed to us : a love episode in the life of a woman who remains essentially unchanged by the experience."

The opening scene shows the garden of the Lerins' country-house. Madame Lerin, seated under the trees, is busy preserving her fruit ; her daughters, Olga and Tatiana, are seen at the open window of the drawing-room. Their duet, " Hearest thou the Nightingale?" is extremely pretty, in a delicate, sentimental style that seems to carry us back to the days of " sensibility " and clear muslin frocks. After the duet comes a quartet, in which Madame Lerin and the old nurse Philipievna take part. Then the peasantry arrive on the scene, and there follows a chorus of harvesters, based on a very original theme, which is quite national in character. At Madame Lerin's invitation they start a choral dance. Meanwhile the sisters come into the garden. Tatiana advances dreamily, book in hand. Olga rallies her sister on her romantic proclivities and sings her first solo, " I have no mind for languor or for sadness," the music of which is in complete contradiction to the words. Their neighbour Lensky, who is in love with Olga, now comes in, and begs permission to introduce his friend Eugene Oniegin. The young men wear high riding-boots and long black cloaks of Byronic fashion. When the young people are left alone, Oniegin entertains Tatiana in a somewhat colourless recitative. After these two have wandered into the garden, Lensky remains with Olga and sings his impassioned love-song, "I love you, Olga." Throughout the entire opera Lensky's music has the most vitality, and is best suited to the character it portrays. Presently the old nurse is sent to announce that tea is served. Her eyes, quickened by love, mark a subtle change in Tatiana. She guesses that her darling has already lost her heart to "the young stranger." As the curtain falls the orchestra, in a few expressive bars, suggests the emotions newly awakened in Tatiana's heart.

In the second scene of the first act, we see Tatiana's room by moonlight. The nurse comes to remind her that it is bed-time. Then there follows a long, confidential recitative between them, while the orchestra carries on a soft accompaniment based upon Tatiana's *Leitmotif*. This scene, so exquisite in every detail—and recalling a similar scene in Shakespeare's *Romeo and Juliet*—is deservedly the most popular number in the whole opera. Tatiana's part is a musical *chef-d'œuvre*, and the nurse's tale, told to an air in the style of a Russian folk-song, is excellent. When the nurse has departed, Tatiana falls into a reverie, from which she rouses to sing her beautiful little song, "Nay, though I be undone," in which she tells her love of Oniegin. But how will he guess her secret, unless she reveals it herself? Then she resolves to write a love-letter to him. Meanwhile the orchestra delicately indicates all the emotions through which Tatiana is passing. Her modesty, her maidenly misgivings, her despair, her ecstasy, and the final triumph of passionate first-love. When the nurse returns, the letter is finished, and Tatiana begs her to convey it to Oniegin. She hesitates, but cannot refuse anything to this child of her heart. As she reluctantly departs on her errand, Tatiana, seated at her writing-table, sinks once more into her dreamy mood, and the curtain falls to her characteristic motive.

The third scene takes us back to the garden of the Lerins' house, and opens with a chorus, based on a folk-song, sung by the peasant girls, who have been gathering berries. As Tatiana enters, the orchestra depicts her ill-concealed agitation. She has not seen the young stranger since she sent her love-letter, and by morning light her conduct seems unmaidenly. Presently Oniegin enters. He cannot appreciate the directness and sweetness of Tatiana's nature. To his jaded mind this simple country-girl is insipid; for he is of the type who finds the savour of love "not in the woman but the chace." He thanks her coldly for her letter, but assures her that he is not a marrying man; and after offering her brotherly affection, gives her some half-cynical advice as to the need of more maidenly reserve in future. Finally he leaves her crushed with shame and the pain of a first disappointment.

The fourth scene opens upon a brilliantly-lighted room in the Lerins' house. The guests are dressed in the quaint costumes and uniforms of the twenties. The ball is in honour of Tatiana's birthday. An old-fashioned slow valse is heard in the orchestra. Oniegin, whom Lensky has dragged to the ball against his will, stands apart from the guests in a mood of cynical boredom. He resolves to console himself by flirting with Olga, and carries her off to dance, leaving Lensky—who is now her accepted lover—fuming with jealousy and injured vanity. Oniegin's music in this scene is probably meant to illustrate his condition of mind, but it leaves an impression of weakness, as well as of coldness, which does not accord with his character. The complimentary couplets to Tatiana, sung to an old-fashioned French air by a typical Frenchman, Triquet, make a pleasant break in the continuous valse-rhythm which accompanies the first part of this scene. After Triquet's solo, the valse gives place to a mazurka, and Olga is again seen dancing and flirting with Oniegin. Lensky loses his self-control, and unwisely demands an explanation. Oniegin is coldly insolent, and Olga rebellious. Lensky first insults his friend, and then forces a challenge upon him. Oniegin now feels some qualms of conscience, but it is too late to retreat or apologise. He consents to go out with Lensky, and the party breaks up in consternation.

The fifth scene represents a winter landscape at dawn. The short orchestral prelude is founded on Lensky's *Leitmotif*, one of the most interesting subjects in the opera. While Lensky is awaiting Oniegin's arrival he sings his aria, "My days of youth, where have they fled?" which is one of the best and most characteristic of Tchaikovsky's inspirations. After the sincere pathos of Lensky's air, the conventional duel scene which follows seems rather poor and stagey.

Some years are supposed to elapse between the fifth and sixth scenes. The curtain rises upon a reception-room in a luxurious house in St. Petersburg. The guests are seen moving to and fro to the music of a brilliant polonaise. Apart from the rest, Oniegin stands in gloomy reflection. In a long and not very interesting recitative he tells of his remorse for Lensky's death, his wanderings in search of peace, and of his jaded spirit, which can find no satisfaction in love or folly. Meanwhile the ball goes on, and the guests are all awaiting the arrival of the acknowledged belle of society, the Princess Gremin. She proves to be Tatiana, grown into a gracious and stately woman of the world. Her husband, Prince Gremin, is a dignified nobleman, high in the diplomatic world, middle-aged, but handsome, and devoted to his beautiful young wife. Oniegin is astonished to recognise in this dazzling woman the girl whose love he had rejected. His chilly egoism is thawed, and he falls passionately in love.

The last scene takes place in the boudoir of Princess Gremin. She is reading a letter from Oniegin. Tatiana has been quietly happy with her elderly prince, but the sight of her first love has awakened her stronger emotions. His letter throws her into a state of agitation, and before she can recover her self-control, Oniegin bursts in upon her with a passionate declaration of love. In a long duet, in which emotion is kept at extreme tension, Oniegin implores her to have pity and to fly with him, while she struggles between honour and reawakened love. Finally, with a supreme effort she breaks away from him at the very moment when she has just confessed her true feeling. When the curtain falls, Oniegin, baffled and despairing, is left alone on the stage.

It would be easy to find fault with the opera of *Eugene Oniegin*, to point to the lack of musical development in the various characters, or to condemn the poverty of the libretto—which, except for a few of Poushkin's original verses—is very poor stuff indeed. But when all is said and done, we are obliged to agree with Berezovsky, that this opera "is like a woman with many faults of heart and character, but whom we love for her beauty in spite of them all."

VII

We have now reached the supreme crisis in the life of Tchaikovsky. At the time of the examinations in May 1877, M. Kashkin thinks the composer was already engaged to be married, although he kept this a secret from all his friends. Afterwards the staff of the Conservatoire dispersed for the summer vacation, and on M. Kashkin's return to Moscow in August, he was considerably surprised at meeting the newly-married couple at a party given in their honour by the Jurgensons. This was the sole occasion upon which M. Kashkin ever saw them together. Tchaikovsky attended to his work at the Conservatoire with his usual regularity, but all his friends observed a change in him. He was reserved and absent-minded, and seemed anxious to avoid all intimate conversation. One day he came to the Conservatoire looking strangely agitated. He said that he had been summoned to St. Petersburg by Napravnik, and took a hasty leave of his colleagues. A few days afterwards the news of his serious illness reached Moscow.

At first the accounts were alarming, but they grew more reassuring after a time. Naturally his sudden departure gave cause for much gossip. Then, as time went on, Tchaikovsky's hasty marriage and its tragic consequences came to be looked upon as an amusing comedy by outsiders. Even his most intimate friends had very little clue to the mysterious catastrophe which seemed to have broken up his life. M. Kashkin, who knew his tender-heartedness and the almost feminine sensibility of his nature, was filled with the gravest apprehensions, which, as it afterwards proved, were not without some foundation. Tchaikovsky afterwards confessed that though he shrank from an act that would have brought public disgrace upon his relatives, he had tried in many ways to shake off the life which was at that time a burden to him, and had gone so far as to stand up to his chest in the river in the first sharp frost of a September night, in the hopes of literally catching his death of cold, and getting rid of his troubles without scandal. Evidently for a short time he was overwrought to the verge of insanity, and owed, perhaps, life and reason to the devoted care of his brother, who took him abroad as soon as his physical condition permitted him to travel. A very peaceful existence in the town of Clarens, on Lake Geneva, did much to restore his health, but his spirit was too bruised to recover quickly. After a short time he wrote to his friends in Moscow that he intended to return to his duties after a long rest, but neither M. Kashkin nor N. Rubinstein thought this at all probable. Some extracts from his letters written at this time will best show his condition of mind during these months of adversity. To Albrecht he writes: " I shall remain abroad the rest of this year (1877), and return about the first of September next year. It is only in absence that one learns to know all the strength of one's affection for one's friends. Now I am living amid the wonderful scenery of Switzerland, and in a week I shall leave here for the still more wonderful beauty of Italy, but my heart belongs undividedly to my dear native land. . . . I am greatly troubled to think that I have put the Conservatoire to inconvenience by my absence . . . but better to be absent for a year than to disappear for ever. Had I stayed a day longer in Moscow, I must have lost my reason and drowned myself in the waves of that stinking—but beloved—Moskva river." To M. Kashkin he writes a little later as follows : " I love Moscow as being the dwelling-place of friends for whom now—in this time of separation— I realise the full strength of my attachment. Physically I am not amiss. Like the old woman in Goburnov's tale, I am sound in one spot while I ache in another. On the whole I am robust ; but as regards my soul, there is a wound there that will never heal. I think I am *homme fini*. Of course I shall return to the Conservatoire on 1st September 1878. As usual I shall take my harmony classes, and shall feel some pleasure in the proximity of my friends ; but what has been can never be again. Something is broken in me ; my wings are cut and I shall never fly very high again. Now I am working hard at *Eugene Oniegin* and my symphony, but I work at the instrumentation of them as though they were written by some one else. . . . It would be too long to tell you all that has happened to me since we parted. My best time was in Clarens, where my brother and I lived very peacefully in absolute solitude amid majestic surroundings. Our going to Italy was pure folly. Her riches, her dazzling luxury, only made me irritable and worried me. I had no heart left to appreciate her great monuments, which left me cold and indifferent."

The stillness of Venice he found comparatively soothing. In Vienna he came once more in contact with his own art, and a little of the old spirit and interest returned to him. In Wagner's *Walkyrie* he took no pleasure ; and speaking of some new work by Brahms, he says that the enthusiasm it aroused among the German critics was incomprehensible to him.

From abroad he sent the first act of *Eugene Oniegin*, and all his friends met to hear it at Rubinstein's rooms. Taneiev played it through on the piano. "The impression was wonderful," says M. Kashkin ; " it fairly took our breath away." Even the critical Nicholas Rubinstein had nothing but praise for the new work. Each time it was played, new beauties revealed themselves, and the wonderful duet between Tatiana and her old nurse made a most favourable impression. Best of all, M. Kashkin felt that it augured happily for his friend's future. This was not the music of an "*homme fini*." By degrees the whole opera arrived, and then some uneasiness was felt as to whether the students of the Conservatoire could possibly create such parts as Tatiana Lerin, Eugene Oniegin, and Vladimir Lensky ; but Tchaikovsky was contented to entrust his work to the students under such leaders as N. Rubinstein and Samarin, rather than let it take the chance of being spoilt by the *routinier* dulness of some theatrical conductor. *Eugene Oniegin* was finished by February 1878, too late for performance during that season, so the composer had to wait, though somewhat impatiently, until the following winter.

In the spring of 1878 it was necessary to appoint some one to take charge of the department of Russian Music at the Paris Exhibition. Both Davidov and N. Rubinstein agreed that Tchaikovsky would be a suitable representative. Tchaikovsky accepted the post, but when he discovered the duties it entailed he hastily resigned it. He had very little capacity for organising, and at that time was absolutely without experience as a conductor, so that his action was undoubtedly a wise one. But Rubinstein, who was a born fighter, and could not understand Tchaikovsky's depression of spirits, nor his shrinking from publicity, was offended at his withdrawal. He believed that he had hit upon a successful plan for curing what he chose to regard as a morbid feeling in Tchaikovsky, and, in a moment of irritation, he reproached him rather severely for his "idleness" and unwillingness to undertake a useful office. This caused a passing coldness between the friends, which was happily soon forgotten. Nicholas Rubinstein ended by going to Paris himself, and he was careful that Tchaikovsky's works should take a prominent place in the programmes of the Russian concerts.

While working at *Eugene Oniegin*, Tchaikovsky had also been engaged upon his *Fourth Symphony*, of which he thought very highly, speaking of it as his best production. Both compositions were sent to Nicholas Rubinstein for performance in Moscow. Rubinstein was usually very successful in his interpretation of Tchaikovsky's music, but, either because his attention was too exclusively taken up with *Eugene Oniegin*, or because this symphony did not appeal to him so strongly as the others, the performance at the Musical Society was slack and colourless. For some years the work was totally neglected, until its revival by Safonov, whose interpretation of it was far better than Rubinstein's.

The *Fourth Symphony* is remarkable for a display of humour somewhat rare in Tchaikovsky's music. Of all the Russian composers he seems the most deficient in this quality. He has not the keen appreciation of national humour which belongs to Glinka. Still less can he make himself one with the peasantry in their noisy revelry, or in their " levity of despair " as Moussorgsky does. Tchaikovsky's humour, as we see it in the *Casse-Noisette Suite*, and other works of a lighter calibre, is always elegant and restrained ; elsewhere it is very fitful, and quickly overcast by the prevailing shadow of his melancholy. But in this symphony it flows more freely, which

seems strange when we remember that he was working at it during a time of great mental depression.
Humour, of a gentle description, peeps out from the
Andante, and becomes more marked and lively in
character in the *Scherzo*, one of the most captivating
movements Tchaikovsky ever wrote. This movement (*Allegro—pizzicato ostinato*) is a rare—if not
unique—instance of a long symphonic movement in
which the strings play pizzicato throughout. The
Finale (*allegro con fuoco*) consists of variations upon
the Russian folk-song, "In the fields there stood a
birch-tree."

The years which followed immediately upon
Tchaikovsky's great domestic trouble were very
fertile in new compositions, and besides those already
mentioned he wrote the music for the *Liturgy of St.
John of Chrysostom* (1878), the *Piano Sonata* (1880),
the *Italian Capriccio* and *Serenade for Strings*, the
Overture 1812, and two sets of songs—all bearing
the dates 1879 and 1880. The *Second Pianoforte
Concerto* also belongs to this period, a work which
presents fewer technical difficulties than the first, but
is still more showy in character.

During the last years of Glinka's life his mind
was very much occupied with national church music,
although his failing health did not permit him to
realise any of the plans he had formed in connection
with these studies. Tchaikovsky was also attracted
by the study of Russian church music, but he wrote
nothing new in this sphere of art. His object was
the same as that of Lvov, who, a few years earlier,

had set himself strenuously to oppose the Italian tendencies which had been introduced by Bortniansky and Berezovsky. In 1875 Tchaikovsky published *A Short Course of Harmony adapted for the Study of Russian Church Music*, which consisted of examples of special difficulties in reading. In 1878 his *Liturgy of St. John of Chrysostom* made its appearance: a service for four voices, in which he keeps rigorously to the old Russian church style, avoiding all western harmonies and forms which are foreign to its spirit. Of the fifteen numbers it contains, the *Credo* is the most remarkable. Berezovsky relates an amusing story connected with this work, which shows the lengths to which Russian officialism can sometimes be carried, even in matters quite unconnected with politics. According to a ukase of Alexander I., all sacred works had to be submitted to the approval of Bortniansky, the intendant of the Imperial Chapel. When Tchaikovsky wrote his Liturgy, Bortniansky had been in his grave for some years. Nevertheless the intendant at that time, Bakhmetiev, refused to take this circumstance into consideration, and confiscated Tchaikovsky's work, on the ground that it had never received Bortniansky's *imprimatur*. Only an order from the chief administration saved the Liturgy from destruction and permitted its publication.

In the spring of 1878 Tchaikovsky returned from abroad, and spent the summer in the country with his relatives. At the close of August—true to his promise—he resumed his duties in Moscow, but not for long. Having enjoyed a whole year of freedom, and known the advantages of unlimited leisure for composition, teaching seemed more irksome than before. Fortunately circumstances now permitted him to resign his classes at the Conservatoire, and early in autumn he went for a short time to Paris. He was, just then, very much preoccupied with the subject of Joan of Arc, and wished to study all that French writers had written about their national heroine.

Meanwhile *Eugene Oniegin* was being studied by the students of the Moscow Conservatoire. "Never was any opera rehearsed with such zeal," says M. Kashkin. Samarin performed wonders in training the pupils, and Nicholas Rubinstein succeeded in putting courage into the hearts of the young singers. A company of experienced artists might have been proud of the results thus achieved. The opera was to be given in March 1879. Tchaikovsky, who had complete confidence in Rubinstein, did not return to Moscow to superintend the rehearsals, but he was expected to be present at the first performance of the work. The actual day of the last rehearsal came, and still the composer had not made his appearance. "I was seated in the amphitheatre," writes M. Kashkin, "the whole theatre being in darkness except for a few candles in the orchestra. Presently I heard some one near to me groping about for a seat, and recognised Tchaikovsky's voice, though he spoke in a whisper. I whispered to him to come and sit near me, and when we met, the heartiness of our embrace caused some scandal in the darkened theatre!" All went smoothly, and the numerous chorus, composed entirely of fresh, young voices, had a wonderful effect. In the scene in which Tatiana writes her love-letter to Oniegin, Tchaikovsky was deeply affected. "How lucky it is dark here," he whispered to his friend, "for this touches me so that I can hardly keep back my tears." No subsequent performance, says M. Kashkin, ever produced so great an impression upon him as this rehearsal. When *Eugene Oniegin* was first performed in the Little Theatre at Moscow, there was an unprecedented crush, and among the audience were Laroche and Anton Rubinstein. The music was of too high an order to be appreciated at a first hearing, and *Oniegin*—like most of Tchaikovsky's works—did not take the audience by storm. Even the St. Petersburg critics spoke coldly of the work, and it was not until five years later that it was heard at the Marinsky Theatre in that town. Time, however, increased its popularity, and when Jurgenson published the pianoforte score, it had an immense sale. Tchaikovsky himself was satisfied with his work, but did not consider it suitable for performance in a large theatre.

From the year 1879 the relations between M. Kashkin and Tchaikovsky became naturally of a less intimate character. Their friendship remained unchanged, but now they only met occasionally, and both being hard workers, their correspondence was restricted to what was absolutely indispensable. *The*

Maid of Orleans was written during the winter of
1879-80.   It was not wanting in touches of genius,
but it was far from being a success.   Speaking of
this opera a year later, Nicholas Rubinstein said that
he considered it a retrograde step from such works
as *Vakoula* and *Eugene Oniegin*.   He believed that
he saw in it a desire to win the public favour, and
added that a mediocre talent might succeed in this
respect, but Tchaikovsky—never.   N. Rubinstein,
in spite of his occasionally severe judgments upon
Tchaikovsky, both as a man and a musician, worked
with untiring energy for the advancement of his
fame.   Of Tchaikovsky's later works, he produced
in Moscow the *First Suite for Orchestra* (op. 43), the
Italian Capriccio and the *Pianoforte Sonata* (op. 37).
With this last work he took immense pains, and it
was long before he was sufficiently pleased with his
own performance to play it in public.   When at last
he resolved to produce it at a concert of the Moscow
Quartet Society, his rendering was so perfect in
every respect that M. Kashkin, unwilling to hear
anything more, left the hall and telegraphed in the
most enthusiastic terms to Tchaikovsky, who was
then living in the country.   In the spring of 1880
Nicholas Rubinstein suggested to Tchaikovsky to
compose a *pièce d'occasion* for the consecration of the
Temple of Christ in Moscow.   Besides the church
festival, Rubinstein wished to organise a musical one
which should embody the history of the building of
this temple, that is to say, the events of the year 1812.
Tchaikovsky's fantasia or overture was to be per-

formed in the public square before the cathedral by a
colossal orchestra, the big drums to be replaced by
salvos of artillery.   The composition entitled *The
Year 1812* was finished at Kamenka in 1880, but
M. Kashkin gives no account of this startling performance.

Tchaikovsky never regarded this work as one of
his best, as we may see from his objections to having
it performed in Berlin during his tour in 1888.   But
the overture has a certain picturesque brilliancy that
raises it above the level of mere sensational music,
and has made it very popular, especially in London.
Berezovsky says it opens with the subject of a
Russian hymn, " God preserve Thy people," and goes
on to represent the Battle of Borodino, in which the
Marseillaise mingles with the Russian national hymn
amid the thunder of artillery.   In using these subjects
Tchaikovsky is guilty of a double anachronism ; for
the Marseillaise was probably not in use in the French
army as late as 1812, while the Russian hymn was
only composed by Lvov in 1863.   The cleverest
effect in the overture is produced by means of a
peal of bells, which very fairly realises the weird
sounds heard in the Kremlin on a Russian feast-day.

As to the merits of the opera *Joan of Arc*, there is
considerable discrepancy of opinion. Some critics by no
means judge it with the severity of Nicholas Rubinstein.   Having never seen this opera, I quote the
following account of it, condensed from Berezovsky.

The Maid of Orleans—as it was finally named—
was produced for the first time on 22nd February 1880,

for the benefit of the conductor of the St. Petersburg opera, Napravnik. The work suffers from a somewhat poor libretto. At times, too, Tchaikovsky seems to be under the influence of Wagner; an influence which is very unsuitable to the particular quality of his genius. As regards the musical presentment of the characters, this opera is far in advance of many others by the same composer. The rôles of Joan, of the King, of Agnes Sorel and Dunois, are all admirably worked out. The remaining characters, such as Joan's parents, Lionel, and the Archbishop, are less developed, but as the interest does not depend upon them, this does not detract from the general effect. But the most prominent feature of the opera is the orchestra, in which Tchaikovsky has centred the chief interest and beauty. He here uses it as the principal medium of expression ; sometimes giving life to the masses, sometimes depicting a spiritual condition. He is equally strong in subtle delineation of character and in broad decorative effects, and in no other opera of Tchaikovsky's is the orchestra called upon to illustrate such depths of thought as in *The Maid of Orleans*.

The opera, which is in four acts, opens with an Introduction consisting of two movements. The first depicts the heroine of the opera ; the second is based on the subject of the chorus of angels, who appear to Joan in her visions, and ends with a cadenza for flute, in imitation of a shepherd's pipe. The first act takes place in Domrémy, while Joan is still living with her parents. The scene of the fire in Domrémy is exceedingly dramatic. So, too, is the chorus of peasants, " O God, stay Thine anger," in which the anguish of the people in this time of calamity is finely expressed. Bertrand's recitative, describing the unhappy condition of France, is the best piece of declamation in the work, especially when sung with feeling. Joan's scene with the populace is somewhat diffuse. The scene ends with an *ensemble*, " King, of power supreme." One of the best numbers in the act is Joan's farewell to her birthplace, which is full of that lyrical sentiment in which Tchaikovsky is always successful.

The angels now appear to Joan, and incite her to great deeds. This chorus, which is accompanied by harps and bells, is exceedingly melodious, and produces a weird effect. The incident of Joan's vision, " Ye host of angels "—the subject of which has already been heard in the Introduction—is a poetical inspiration. The orchestra describes Joan's condition of mind : a sort of mystical ecstasy leading on to inspired action. This scene closes the first act.

The entr'acte which precedes Act II. is not very striking from a musical point of view. The curtain rises upon a room in the palace of Charles VII., where the king is shown in the midst of frivolous gaiety. The beautiful subject of the minstrel's song recalls the style of a Malo-Russian melody. The gipsy dance is effective as regards orchestration, but lacks colour. The ballet which follows—a dance of pages and dwarfs, and a jester's dance—is not specially French in character, but it is splendidly orchestrated.

In the duet between the king and "le brave Dunois" both characters are convincingly portrayed. We recognise the superficial, effeminate disposition of the former, and the contrasting energy and virility of the latter. Towards the close, the duet works up to an effective crescendo, and ends with an accompaniment of drums in the orchestra. The subject of Agnes Sorel's air, "If strength be not given thee," is slightly Russian in style. The duet between Agnes and the king is also an excellent piece of character drawing. The orchestral music which announces the entrance of Joan is very impressive. Then follows a fine scene in which she is questioned by the king and relates her story, beginning, "Holy Father, I am called Joan." This tale is sincere, naïve, and full of sentiment, and is the best number of this act. With the mention of the Holy Virgin, there is a passage in the orchestra for harps. Only a slight diffuseness spoils this narrative. The recitative which precedes the final *ensemble* is poor, but the *ensemble* itself is grandiose and effective.

The third act is divided into two scenes or tableaux. The introduction to the first represents a battle. The love-episode between Joan and Lionel is very weak. Lionel is altogether lacking in character, and Joan's recitative—in the Italian style — is not expressive. The duet "Dread Powers" is the best part of the scene. The arrival of Dunois, whose personality is always well defined, offers a strong contrast to what has gone before. The second scene takes place at Rheims, and musically is the most effective in the whole opera. It opens with a Coronation March, repeated three times, and rather noisy as regards instrumentation. The duet (recitative) between Joan's father and mother is rather long and monotonous. The father, deaf to his wife's admonitions and prayers, resolves to denounce his daughter before the king and the populace. The scene which follows is highly dramatic. The actual denunciation is preceded by a short chorus in march rhythm. Both the king's speech and that of Joan's father are characteristic. The accompaniments are somewhat heavy, but throughout the entire act the orchestra is very prominent. The *Finale* is on a grand scale, and if given without cuts, would be almost equal to one-fourth of the whole opera.

The fourth act is preceded by an orchestral entr'acte, which illustrates Joan's mystical frame of mind. This instrumental piece reflects all that is best in Tchaikovsky's genius, and is one of the most successful things in the work. The first scene opens with a short recitative for Joan. Lionel then appears, and there follows a very fine love-scene, ending in a great duet. In the middle of this duet the choir of angels is heard, reminding Joan of her duty and predicting her ruin. But love prevails. Joan does not heed the warning voices, and disaster is already at hand. The English soldiers break in upon the lovers, and after slaying Lionel, take Joan prisoner.

The last scene of the opera—Joan's execution—opens with a Funeral March, to the strains of which she is led to the market-place. In a beautiful recitative she commends her soul to heaven, and is answered by the choir of angels. The maid is then led to the stake, and a great chorus, with most expressive orchestral accompaniment, completes this opera, which, says Berezovsky, is one of the most brilliant creations of Tchaikovsky's genius.

VIII

IN 1880 Nicholas Rubinstein's health was failing rapidly, but almost his last visit to the Conservatoire was made on behalf of his friend. He took a great interest in the *Serenade* (op. 48), and wishing to get a general idea of the work, ordered the parts to be copied, assembled the students' orchestra, and though he was too ill to stand at the conductor's desk, managed to go through the work in a sitting posture. Shortly after this he went to Paris, where he died on 11th March 1881. The death of this great artist, and devoted friend, was a heavy blow to Tchaikovsky. During the following year he appears to have written only one work—the *Pianoforte Trio in A minor*, dedicated "to the memory of a great artist," and inscribed *Roma*, Gennaio, 1882. The name of Rubinstein was not mentioned in the inscription, because Tchaikovsky desired less to honour his friend than the artist for whom he felt a boundless veneration. As Tchaikovsky had long cherished a prejudice against the combination of piano and stringed instruments, it is interesting to hear his own reasons, as given to M. Kashkin, for his choice on this occasion. In the first place, he said that he would not dream of writing anything in memory of so great a pianist in which the piano did not take a prominent part. Then, again, a concerto or fantasia seemed to him too extravagant and showy a form in which to embody his idea; while the pianoforte alone seemed too monotonous and thin for the purpose. He decided, therefore, in favour of the trio. In the second movement of the work appear the variations in which are embodied Tchaikovsky's memories of Nicholas Rubinstein and his musical characteristics at various periods of his life. "It would be possible," says M. Kashkin, "to label each of these variations with an appropriate title; but I prefer to do this elsewhere."

From 1882-83 Tchaikovsky was chiefly engaged upon the opera *Mazeppa*. The first performances of this work were fixed for almost the same night in both capitals, and Tchaikovsky chose to be present at Moscow rather than at St. Petersburg. All went exceedingly well, and the opera had even a brilliant success, but Tchaikovsky's nervous temperament made rehearsals and "first nights" a torture to him. Every one was pleased but the composer himself, who looked "like a condemned criminal," and seemed on the verge of an hysterical attack. The following evening his *Second Suite for Orchestra* was to be played for the first time at a concert of the Musical Society, but when the audience called loudly for the composer he was not forthcoming, being at that time half-way to Smolensk. Tchaikovsky, unable to endure another ovation, had fled from Moscow, leaving M. Kashkin to make his excuses to the conductor and the public. The libretto of *Mazeppa*, taken from Poushkin's poem *Poltava*, is the joint work of several collaborators, among them the well-known writer Bourenin. The librettists have evidently been anxious to keep as many episodes as possible from the original work, without reference to their fitness for scenic representation. The result is a series of gloomy pictures, prison scenes, executions, deaths, etc., which cannot fail to have a very depressing effect upon the audience. The music of *Mazeppa* is unequal, but, generally speaking, the instrumental parts of the opera are superior to the vocal. The style of the vocal portion is patchy, alternately Russian and Italian, sometimes a little German as regards the recitatives. The scene of the opera is laid chiefly in the Ukraine, and it is remarkable that Tchaikovsky has not been very successful in his use of local colour, for there is nothing distinctively Malo-Russian about the songs and dances of the Cossacks in *Mazeppa*. The hero of the opera is not represented in romantic colours, but appears as an ambitious, sly, and treacherous soldier of fortune. This is Poushkin's presentment of the celebrated hetman of Cossacks, and no doubt, historically, it is the correct one.

The opera opens with an Introduction, and the curtain rises upon the estate of the Cossack chief,

Kochoubey, a wealthy land-owner and judge. Kochoubey's daughter, Marie, is beloved by a young Cossack named Andrew, but she has lost her heart to the great hetman Mazeppa, who is much older than herself. Mazeppa is being entertained by Kochoubey. There is a characteristic chorus of Cossacks, followed by a local dance, the gopak. During the process of the dance, Mazeppa asks for Marie's hand, and is refused. This causes a breach between Kochoubey and the hetman. Marie clings to her lover, and finally goes off with him. In the second scene, which takes place in Kochoubey's house, every one is lamenting the departure of Marie. Her father is heartbroken. But her mother, with true Cossack sternness, bids her husband "cease this grieving," and urges him to action. Kochoubey and his followers decide to denounce Mazeppa to Peter the Great. Andrew is chosen to carry the accusation.

The second act reveals the dungeons of the tower of Bielotserkovsky, where Kochoubey, who has been captured by Mazeppa, is languishing in chains and threatened with torture. The scene is exceedingly gloomy, and the actual preparations for the torturing of the prisoner are gruesome; but from a musical point of view the scene has some fine moments. Berezovsky considers that this scene, together with Tatiana's scene in the second act of *Eugene Oniegin*, are Tchaikovsky's *chefs-d'œuvre*, and display his power of psychological analysis at its highest. The second scene of this act opens with a fine monologue for Mazeppa. It is first descriptive of the lovely, soft night of the Ukraine, and then of Mazeppa's inward agitation. Orlik, Mazeppa's follower, now comes in bearing the order for Kochoubey's execution, which the hetman has treacherously secured. Presently Marie comes upon the scene. In the love-duet which follows, Mazeppa reveals something of the treachery at work in his mind, but Marie is absorbed in her love and suspects none of the plots against her father. When Mazeppa leaves her she sings a love-song, which is very Italian in character, but expresses her condition of mind. Her mother breaks in upon her and tells her of Mazeppa's cruelty and falseness towards her father. A military march is heard in the distance. It is Kochoubey being led to execution. The women hear it, and are overcome with despair.

The scene of the execution follows. A crowd has collected in the field, where a scaffold has been erected for Kochoubey and his companion Iskra. The whole scene is gloomy and unpleasantly realistic, especially the chorus of drunken Cossacks, "Ho, get along." The farewell of the condemned men to the populace and their prayer are very dramatic. The latter, says Berezovsky, is based on church tones. The loud chord in the orchestra which announces that the prisoners' heads have fallen is a piece of sensationalism which has its parallel in Richard Strauss's symphonic poem *Till Eulenspiegel*, where a hideous discord informs the audience that "the drop" has been rightly judged and "death was instantaneous," as the reporters say.

Marie and her mother arrive at the foot of the scaffold too late to save Kochoubey or say a last farewell. The last scene is ushered in by a descriptive orchestral number entitled "The Battle of Poltava." Two subjects are employed: one the melody of a national song, "Glory" ("Slavsia"); the other a march of the period of Peter the Great. The action returns to Kochoubey's estate, now ruined and deserted. Andrew, who has been wandering in search of Mazeppa with the intention of killing him, comes back to the homestead. In the orchestra some phrases of the first duet, between Andrew and Marie, recall the happy days of prosperity before Mazeppa appeared on the scene. Presently the hetman and his follower Orlik come on. Andrew throws himself upon Mazeppa, but the latter draws his pistol and fires upon the young Cossack. Marie now appears. Her grief has unhinged her mind. She sings a duet with Mazeppa which is not particularly expressive, but the orchestral accompaniment, in which the theme of the love-duet in the second act is ingeniously brought in, supplements the dramatic feeling and reminds us of her past love for the treacherous hetman. When Mazeppa and Orlik have gone away, abandoning the poor crazy girl to her fate, one of the most pathetic and dramatic scenes in the opera is enacted. Marie is now left alone with Andrew. Her duet with the dying Cossack is full of sentiment, but the supreme touch of pathos is felt when she unconsciously lulls her former lover into the sleep of death with her graceful, innocent slumber-song. The chorus of the people, with which the opera concludes, comes as an anticlimax after this very moving incident.

Tchaikovsky's *Third Orchestral Suite* was finished in July 1884, and during the second half of the summer, while on a visit to the beautiful estate of Plestcheevo, he began to work upon the fantasia for orchestra, *Manfred*. The subject had been suggested to him by Balakirev, but it did not suit his particular genius as well as *Romeo and Juliet*. He never seems to have been possessed by his subject, and the composition was only achieved by dint of strenuous efforts. "*Manfred* cost me a whole year of my life," he once said to M. Kashkin ; and even in the opinion of his friend it does not compare at all favourably with Schumann's treatment of the same subject.

Manfred is described as "a symphony in four scenes," and its programme is based on Byron's poem, with this difference, that Tchaikovsky's Manfred does not die a haughty but sublime rebel, like Byron's hero, but is finally reconciled to Heaven. The programme of the symphony stands as follows :—

First movement or scene. "Manfred wandering amid the Alpine heights. Worn out with fruitless questioning of Fate, torn by tortures of despair and the memory of his guilty past, he endures intolerable anguish of soul. Manfred has penetrated deeply into the mysteries of witchcraft, and associated with the powers of evil; but neither they, nor any-

thing else in the world, can give him the boon of
forgetfulness which he is always vainly seeking and
imploring. The remembrance of the dead Astarte,
once so passionately loved, gnaws at his heart, and
there is no limit or end to Manfred's despair." This
movement affords great scope for varied emotional
treatment. Manfred is alternately racked with
anguish, or lost in the memory of his past love.
Throughout the scene we hear the love - subject,
detached like a shimmering streak of moonlight upon
a black and fathomless pool.

The second scene may be considered in the light
of a *scherzo*, and has the following title : "The spirit
of the Alps appears to Manfred in the rainbow over
the waterfall." The third scene is described as "A
picture of the simple but prosperous life of the
mountaineers." It is pastoral in character, but amid
the joyous and peaceful strains of the shepherds'
pipes we hear the sinister subject which represents
Manfred.

The final tableau is entitled, "The subterranean
palace of Arimane. Orgy of evil spirits. Manfred
appears at the bacchanalian revels. The invocation
and apparition of the spirit of Astarte. She predicts
the end of his sufferings on earth. Manfred's
death." The orgy is not particularly impressive.
The subject is more suited to a Berlioz or a Moussorgsky than to the more delicate lyricism of
Tchaikovsky. The death of Manfred brings a
reference to the *Dies Irae* of the Greek Church. At
the close of the movement there is a return to the

first subject of the *Finale* in D (with organ accompaniment). This probably represents the redemption of Manfred.

Composed at a somewhat later date than *Manfred*, and allied to it, if not in musical structure at least as regards its psychological basis, is the fantasia-overture *Hamlet*. The music of *Hamlet* is chiefly based on three themes : the sombre one, appropriate to the hero ; a contrasting theme, pathetic and graceful, associated with Ophelia ; and one which has the character of a march. The subject ought to have been congenial to Tchaikovsky's temperament, and yet it is impossible to look upon this work as one of his greatest successes. It seems as though he had set himself to realise too minutely the interminable agitations and misgivings which beset the prince. He has approached the play from the psychological rather than the dramatic side, and the result is a work of inordinate length, with few salient emotional crises and much that is vague and impossible to realise convincingly in music. That *Hamlet* exercised a fascination upon Tchaikovsky seems evident from the fact that before composing this fantasia-overture he had already written incidental music to the play, consisting in all of fifteen numbers. Of these the Overture, Elegy, three scenes for Ophelia, and the Gravedigger's Song are the most interesting.

IX

TCHAIKOVSKY was now able to realise his ideal of a quiet life, spent chiefly in the country. In 1885 he took a house in the village of Maidanovo, not far from the little town of Klin. Maidanovo was a pretty village, close to a luxuriant park, with a good bathing-place and many rural attractions. It had, unfortunately, one supreme drawback. In summertime the neighbouring houses were let to families from the city, who brought with them the inevitable piano, and soon the sounds of scales and exercises reached the unfortunate composer at his work. In consequence of this, Tchaikovsky moved into another house outside the park, enclosed in its own grounds and beyond reach of his neighbours' music. Here he would spend months together without visiting the town. His intimate friends were welcome at Maidanovo, but they respected the solitude of " The Hermit of Klin," as they called him. From time to time, as a work was finished, or Tchaikovsky felt the need of a rest, he would invite a party of musical friends from Moscow for a night or two. M. Kashkin was often privileged to stay on by himself for a longer visit at Maidanovo. Very simple, strictly regulated, and calm was this country life. The two friends breakfasted at eight. At nine they separated for the morning, which was spent in work. At one o'clock came a simple, early dinner of two courses (Tchaikovsky kept a good man-cook, and could entertain his guests lavishly enough when he thought it necessary), and then followed a long country walk, which the composer never missed in any weather. Sometimes Tchaikovsky would announce at dinner his intention of going out alone, and then his friend understood that he was meditating some new creation, for many of his works were planned and his themes invented during these long solitary rambles across country. After tea he went back to his work until supper was served at eight o'clock. After supper the servant put a bottle of wine on the table, and was told that he was free until the next morning. "Left to ourselves we immediately went to the piano," writes M. Kashkin, "and began to play arrangements for four hands, of which Tchaikovsky had a large store. Often we played Brahms, whom he esteemed very highly for his seriousness and sincerity, and his contempt for superficial success ; but at the same time he had not much sympathy with his music, finding it cold and dry." Even after repeatedly playing Brahms's works his first impression was not greatly modified. Occasionally the occupation was varied by M. Kashkin's reading aloud some of

Tchaikovsky's favourite Russian authors ; or the composer would write up his diary, of which he possessed many bound volumes, the contents of which were never revealed even to his closest friends. That it contained many intimate things as regards himself, besides the secrets of others, there can be no doubt. Once, he told M. Kashkin, he was spending the evening quite alone at his country house. As his eye fell upon the volumes of his diary he was assailed by a sudden terror lest he might die with no friends at hand, and that some one should pry into these life-secrets. Under the influence of this feeling, he immediately ordered his fire to be lit, and burnt every volume before he went to bed. There was much in it which he regretted, but on the whole he believed that he had acted wisely.

Tchaikovsky had very little idea of the value of money. On one occasion a friend inquired : " Peter Ilich, where do you invest your capital ? " Tchaikovsky stared at him in astonishment, and then burst out laughing. It had never occurred to him that there was any possible investment of capital otherwise than in personal expenditure and presents to friends. Breathless with laughter, he explained to his friend that his last investment of capital had been in the hotel where he had stayed at Moscow ; " and where my next investment may be, I am sure I cannot tell you at present."

In the country he spoilt all the peasant children by giving them coppers. Taneiev and Kashkin reproached him for this bad habit, saying that it demoralised the children, and using other virtuous arguments. The next time they went for a walk, Tchaikovsky resolved to make an heroic effort to escape from the youthful beggars whose morals were corrupted by his kopecks. They started for the bridge which crosses the river on the road to Klin. Tchaikovsky's hour for walking was known to every child in the neighbourhood, and feeling sure that he would be waylaid on leaving the park, he tried to deceive his persecutors. Leaving Taneiev and Kashkin on the path, he descended to the river-bank and crept under the thick sallow-bushes, while Taneiev, from the upper road, watched his furtive movements, and recited with mock pathos, " Behold the worthy fruits of evil-doing," etc. Tchaikovsky's innocent ruse availed him nothing. The children, who had studied the character of their victim to some purpose, had posted sentries in ambush, and by the time Tchaikovsky reached the bridge a party of boys were awaiting him. His friends came up just in time to hear the joyful laughter of the victorious enemy as they moved off laden with booty. Tchaikovsky, blushing with confusion, hastened to explain that he really could not help it, that he had given the children the merest trifle, etc. M. Kashkin did not quite believe in this extenuating circumstance. On one occasion Tchaikovsky had given away at least fourteen shillings in an afternoon's walk, and, in addition, had borrowed all that his friend had with him at the moment.

The chief works of 1886 and 1887 comprise an

opera, *Charodaïka* ("The Sorceress"), *Dumka*, a rural scene for orchestra, a number of songs, the *Fourth Orchestral Suite* ("Mozartiana"), a *Pezzo Capriccioso* for violoncello and orchestra, and the *Fifth Symphony*.

It will be a matter of surprise to many to find that Berezovsky ranks the last-named work lower than the *Fourth Symphony*, whereas in England many critics have pronounced it to be almost, if not quite, equal to "The Pathetic." But Berezovsky's account of the work, in spite of his critical judgment upon it, is so interesting that I give it here in full. "The *Fifth Symphony*," he writes, "is the weakest of all Tchaikovsky's symphonies; nevertheless it is a striking work, and takes a prominent place not only among Tchaikovsky's compositions, but among Russian musical works in general. The symphony is divided into the usual four movements. The first—*Andante, Allegro con anima*—opens with an introduction in which we hear the exposition of the chief subject of the symphony. This subject runs like a dark thread through the whole tissue of the work. The introduction is conceived in that mood of sadness so common to Tchaikovsky. The *Allegro* has two subjects: one melancholy in character, the other full of brightness and vitality. Both are developed with much brilliance and animation. Then, suddenly, the chief subject reappears and the music grows sombre once more. As this theme dies away on the bassoons, the movement comes to an end. The second movement—*Andante cantabile con alcuna licenza*—takes the form of a romance.

The subject given out by a solo horn passes over to the violoncello, and is afterwards assigned to the strings. Here again the chief theme of the symphony breaks in in a fragmentary, almost unexpected, manner, casting momentary shadows over the radiant mood which pervades the movement. The third movement consists of a poetical, graceful valse. As in the preceding movement, the chief theme returns occasionally in a fitful way ; but later on, in the *Finale*, it is displayed in its fullest power. The introduction to the *Finale*—*Andante maestoso*—is entirely based upon it, and is penetrated with religious feeling. The *Finale* itself (*Allegro vivace*) grows gradually clearer as it proceeds, as though the heart had cast off a load of suffering and God's world shone out bright once more. An episode in the *Finale* has a subject which is quite Russian in character. The entire symphony seems to set forth some dark spiritual experience, some heavy condition of a mind torn by importunate memories which have poisoned existence. Only at the close the clouds lift, the sky clears, and we see the blue stretching pure and clear beyond."

When Tchaikovsky left Maidanovo, he moved to the old manor-house of Frovolo, which was also situated in the neighbourhood of Klin. Here Kashkin was an occasional visitor. On the completion of his opera *The Queen of Spades*, the composer invited a large party of friends, chiefly from the Moscow Conservatoire, to hear the new work. The subject of the opera was borrowed from a tale by Poushkin, and a great part of it was composed during a visit to Italy. On the occasion of the trial of *The Queen of Spades* at Frovolo, Siloti took the piano part. The libretto was prepared by the composer's brother, Modeste Ilich Tchaikovsky, and differs considerably from Poushkin's original story.

Herman, a needy young lieutenant, a moody hero of the Byronic school, falls in love with Lisa, a beautiful orphan who lives with her grandmother. The old Countess has been celebrated in her day as "The Venus of Moscow," and equally noted as an inveterate card-player. Herman is also passionately fond of gaming, so much so that he hardly knows which fascinates him most—his love of Lisa or his love of the cards. Lisa is very much attracted by the young man's interesting melancholy, but she is affianced to Prince Yeletsky, a richer and more desirable match. Herman wishes to make a fortune at cards in order to win the woman of his heart. There is an ugly story to the effect that the Countess owes her luck at cards to some supernatural agency. Herman sets himself to fathom this mystery, but manages so clumsily that the old lady dies of fright without having revealed her secret. After death she revenges herself. Her ghost appears to Herman, and whispers the names of three cards which he imagines to be her lucky ones. On these cards he stakes his all, is ruined, and stabs himself.

The subject of *The Queen of Spades* has some points of resemblance with that of *Eugene Oniegin*, but the music has not the freshness, the lyrical charm, or the pathos of Tchaikovsky's earlier opera. It was originally written for another libretto, based upon Poushkin's story "The Captain's Daughter"; but after working at this subject for some time, Tchaikovsky, for some unexplained reason, changed his mind, and used up his material for *The Queen of Spades*.

Tchaikovsky's last effort in dramatic music was the one-act opera *Iolanthe*, on the subject of Herz's drama, "King Réné's Daughter." It is generally considered to be the weakest of his operatic works.

Very superior, in its own way, is the music of a ballet, in thirty numbers, *The Sleeping Beauty*. This charming new setting of an old story is one of Tchaikovsky's most delicate and graceful inspirations. The music, though not deeper than the subject demands, is melodious in the best sense of the word, fantastic, brightly coloured; while it never descends to the commonplace level of the ordinary ballet music. Another work of this description which appeared in 1892 has won extraordinary popularity in this country—the *Casse-Noisette*. This was originally written as a fairy ballet in fifteen numbers, from which Tchaikovsky afterwards arranged the Suite which is so often heard at the Queen's Hall and elsewhere, and of which the English public never seems to have had enough.

Among Tchaikovsky's last works was the *Sextet for Strings* ("Souvenir de Florence"), dedicated to the St. Petersburg Chamber Music Society. M. Kashkin, who was staying with Tchaikovsky while he was engaged upon this, says that at first the composer found it extremely difficult, but after a few days he declared he had quite solved the mysterious art of writing for this special combination of instruments—two violins, two alti, and two violoncellos. But the result showed that even a very experienced musician may sometimes fail to realise the effect of what he has put on paper. Kashkin writes : "The first movement of the sextet, with its second theme —in character resembling a broad Italian *cantilena*— did not present any special difficulties, as it approached more nearly to symphonic form than to chamber music. In the remaining movements the composer endeavoured to keep strictly to chamber-music form, and had recourse to contrapuntal combinations, which gave each instrument its full independence and equality with the others." When the two musicians tried it on the piano for four hands they were delighted with the effect ; especially with the two fugues for six voices, which seemed to them entirely successful. Tchaikovsky determined to hear the work played by stringed instruments before sending it to the publisher, and despatched it to Albrecht, in Petersburg, to have the parts copied. Albrecht was very enthusiastic, and declared it would rank among the first works of its kind. For some time M. Kashkin heard no more of the sextet, and on inquiring what had become of it, Tchaikovsky informed him that at the trial much of it had proved quite impracticable, especially the fugues which had pleased them so much. The crossing of the parts with instruments of uniform *timbre* made it impossible to follow the independent movement of the voices in the counterpoint, and produced some very ugly harmonies. The sextet in its present amended form was not published until 1892.

To those who understood Tchaikovsky's sensitive shrinking from publicity, the alacrity with which, during the last years of his life, he accepted engagements to conduct his own works, was a problem beyond solution. According to his own account, he took no pleasure in conducting, and was always relieved when the task was over. When responsible for the works of others, Kashkin says his anxiety was so acute that his face wore "an expression of physical pain." His renown as a composer gave him some weight as a conductor, which he was unable to profit by to any great extent. On his tours abroad he was occasionally very successful with his own works, but he had not the temperament which finds pleasure in applause. There seems to be little doubt that many of his compositions suffered from his resolve to conduct the first performance of them himself. This was the case with his *Fifth Symphony*, written in 1888, and published the following year. For some years after its first production the symphony was scarcely heard a second time, and Tchaikovsky was so discouraged by the coldness of the public and the critics that, had it not been already published, it would undoubtedly have shared the fate of his earlier works *Undine* and *Fatum*. It was revived by Nikisch with brilliant success in 1895. The same cause— his rather easy-going and inanimate style of conducting—brought about the failure of his orchestral ballade *The Voievoda*, which composition he actually did burn on the night of its first performance.

M. Kashkin gives an amusing account of the meeting between Brahms and Tchaikovsky at Hamburg, where the latter had gone to conduct his *Fifth Symphony*. They had met two years earlier in Leipzig, but Brahms journeyed to Hamburg on purpose to hear the new symphony. After the concert he invited the Russian composer to dine with him, and after entertaining him most hospitably, he confided to him with quiet sincerity that he did not like the symphony at all. He spoke so simply that Tchaikovsky did not feel in the least hurt, only he was encouraged to speak out with the same uncompromising sincerity his own convictions about the work of the great German master. They parted excellent friends ; but never had another opportunity of meeting.

Tchaikovsky, although he gave no impression of great physical strength, was wiry and not easily fatigued. He had lived simply, and hardened himself by taking outdoor exercise at all seasons of the year. Nevertheless, at fifty he began to show some signs of the troubles he had suffered and the hard mental work he had accomplished. He could no longer give himself up so entirely to composition ; he needed more rest and distraction, and unfortunately his sight began to be affected. He could no longer read with comfort, and thus he was deprived of one of his chief sources of occupation during the long evenings which he spent alone in his country house. He had left the manor-house of Frovolo and taken up his residence nearer to Klin itself. Four years before his death he was appointed one of the directors of the Moscow Musical Society, and considered it his duty to remain in the city during the concert season. But town life, with its constant succession of visitors, and other encroachments upon his time, was very distasteful to him, and he was relieved when his conscience allowed him to give up his rooms there and return to the solitude of Klin. That he preferred it to any other life seems beyond a doubt, but there is something rather pathetic in M. Kashkin's picture of the "Hermit of Klin," touched—however lightly —with the infirmities of age and of a strenuous existence, sitting by his solitary fire, longing, as he sometimes said, "for my three rubbers" which he could not get, and consoling himself with a game of patience, or with the score of some new work which had awakened his interest. To have made friends with his neighbours would have been to surrender his complete liberty and lay himself open to interruption at inconvenient times. His art demanded the sacrifice of the social life.

The *Sixth Symphony*, to which, after its first performance, Tchaikovsky gave the title of "The Pathetic," was sketched out early in 1893, and finished a few months later, on his return from his last tour abroad. It bears the date of 31st August 1893. The work is so well known, and has been so frequently analysed, that it is superfluous to go into

further details about it here.   But a few words may
be said as to the circumstances under which it was
written, and the feelings that inspired it.   Each of
Tchaikovsky's symphonies has a definite colouring
which shows the prevailing influence under which it
was written.   The Second shows us the composer
still strongly dominated by national tendencies.   The
Third is tinctured throughout by his increasing eclecticism in general, and in particular by his newly
awakened enthusiasm for Schumann.   The Fourth is
remarkable for its brighter qualities, and especially
for its unwonted display of humour.   The Fifth has
touches of religious feeling which are absent from all
the rest.   In the Sixth, Tchaikovsky seems to have
concentrated the brooding melancholy which is the
most characteristic and recurrent of all his emotional
phases.   Throughout the whole of his music we are
never far away from this shadow.   Sometimes this
mood seems real enough ; sometimes it strikes us as
merely artificial and rhetorical.   But melancholy in
some form constitutes the peculiar quality of his
genius, and nowhere does it brood more heavily or
with more tragic intensity than in the last movement
of this symphony.

There is no doubt that one of the reasons of the
extraordinary popularity of this work lies in the fact
that it has been invested with an autobiographical
interest for which there is no real warranty.   It is
said that in some vague and mysterious way it fore-
shadowed the composer's approaching end.   Perhaps
it is also with the idea of supporting this theory that

sensationalists have discovered that Tchaikovsky shortly afterwards committed suicide. The idea is picturesque, but neither in Russia nor abroad have I discovered any substantial ground for the report. At the time of writing the *Sixth Symphony*, Tchaikovsky had passed through his dark hour and won his way back to the light. M. Kashkin distinctly explodes "the pathetic fallacy," if I may so far distort the meaning of Ruskin's phrase. He shows that the work was not composed under the influence of a morbid pre-occupation with death. Tchaikovsky had some idea of writing out the programme of the symphony, but never did so, chiefly because no sooner was it finished than he became absorbed in new plans, of which the remodelling of *The Oprichnik* was one. Had he done so, the world would not have found that the symphony was a kind of legacy to the living from one who was filled with a presentiment of his own approaching end. It seems, then, more reasonable to interpret both the overwhelming energy of the third movement, and the abysmal sorrow of the *Finale*, in the broader light of a national or historical signifi-cance, rather than to narrow them to the expression of an individual experience. If the last movement is intended to be predictive, it is surely of things vaster, and issues more fatal, than are contained in a mere personal apprehension of death. It speaks rather of a "*lamentation large et souffrance inconnue*," and seems to set the seal of finality on all human hopes. Even if we eliminate the purely subjective interest, this autumnal inspiration of Tchaikovsky's, in which we hear "the groundwhirl of the perished leaves of hope," still remains the most profoundly stirring of his works. Less artistically perfect than those glowing summer blossoms of his genius *Romeo and Juliet* and *Francesca di Rimini*, the *Sixth Symphony*, with its strange combination of the mediocre and the sublime, is profoundly human. Few works have awakened such an immediate echo in the heart of the public. It is interesting to know that he himself had no misgivings about the first three movements of the symphony, but thought it not improbable that, after its first performance in St. Petersburg, he might have to rewrite the *Finale.*[1]

During the spring and summer of 1893 Kashkin and Tchaikovsky never met; but on 7th October the latter returned to Moscow, partly in order to attend the funeral of a very dear friend—Zoeriev. On the 9th, Tchaikovsky attended the Conservatoire to hear a vocal quartet of Mozart's for which he had written the words, and in the evening he invited M. Kashkin to dine with him at the Moscow Hotel. Pollini, the conductor of the Hamburg opera, and Safonov were of the party. During dinner the talk was of a business character, Pollini being anxious to make a tour through Russia with a German orchestra, engaging Tchaikovsky and Safonov as conductors.

[1] I have the best authority for stating that this symphony was not specially commissioned by any musical society in Russia or abroad. Tchaikovsky had a great objection to composing to order, a custom which was not in agreement with his artistic views. The *Sixth Symphony* is dedicated to his favourite nephew M. V. Davidov.

After dinner M. Kashkin was left alone with his friend. They had much to talk about after their long separation. Tchaikovsky told of his visit to Cambridge, when he received his doctor's degree, and spoke in kindly remembrance of the hospitality offered to him there, and particularly of the Professor who had taken him into his own house. He also spoke of Arrigo Boïto, who had charmed him with his wit and culture. Then they took up a sadder theme—the death of their intimate friends, Albrecht and Zoeriev. Their particular circle was growing narrow. Who would be the next to go ? M. Kashkin, half joking, said that Tchaikovsky would be the last ; and he answered in the same tone that it was not unlikely, for he had never felt better or happier in his life. Tchaikovsky had to catch the night mail to St. Petersburg, where he was going to conduct his *Sixth Symphony*, and so the friends parted, without the least presentiment that it was for the last time.

There was a concert of the Musical Society fixed for 12th October, and Tchaikovsky intended to return to Moscow in time for it, and invited M. Kashkin to dine with him in the evening to meet the singer, Eugene Oudin. At the concert M. Kashkin looked for his friend, and he then heard, for the first time, that a telegram had been received announcing Tchaikovsky's illness, but stating that the danger was over. The telegram was hardly understood by his friends, who, not being sure of his address, decided to telegraph to the St. Petersburg

Conservatoire. But it was Sunday, so the message lay unanswered until the next day, when the announcement of Tchaikovsky's death appeared in the Moscow *Viedomosti*. M. Kashkin at once left for St. Petersburg, but there he learnt the sad circumstances of the case. Tchaikovsky had died of cholera ; the preparations for the funeral were made in haste, and he had not even the sad consolation of seeing his friend's face again.

M. Kashkin concludes his book with the following somewhat enigmatical passage, which probably refers to the unhappy circumstances of Tchaikovsky's marriage :—

"I have now finished my reminiscences. Of course they might be supplemented by a few more events, but I shall add nothing at present, and perhaps I shall never do so. One document I shall leave in a sealed packet, and if thirty years hence it still has any interest for the world, the seal may be broken ; this packet I shall leave to the care of the Moscow Conservatoire. It will contain the history of one episode in Tchaikovsky's life upon which I have only touched in my book."

Upon this episode I am not able to throw any further light. When the authorised life and correspondence of the composer appears, his relatives may possibly clear up the mystery which surrounds it. On the other hand, it is more than probable that they will not take the public into their confidence upon a subject about which Tchaikovsky himself preserved an almost unbroken reticence.

TCHAIKOVSKY AS A MUSICAL CRITIC

THERE are certain books which owe their prestige more to the personality of their authors than to their intrinsic literary value. To this class belongs *The Collected Writings of Tchaikovsky*, edited, with a preface, by his friend and colleague G. A. Laroche. Such books, although devoted to special subjects, generally command a wide public. For though it may be true, as Tchaikovsky himself says, that great composers are rarely gifted with an infallible critical instinct, the majority will always pause to hear a great artist speaking of his own art rather than listen to the voice of the professional critic, prose he never so wisely.

Tchaikovsky's career as a musical writer was brief. He undertook the work rather from necessity than from inclination, and, regarding it as an unwelcome interruption in his busy, creative life, he gladly laid aside his pen when circumstances permitted him to do so. His literary legacy cannot be

compared in importance and interest with those of
Schumann, Liszt, or Berlioz. It is chiefly valuable
because it throws a narrow shaft of light upon his
personal tastes and the tendencies which influenced
his music; subjects which Tchaikovsky generally
kept in modest obscurity. It is evident that his own
ideal in criticism was something strictly impersonal
and objective, "a system founded on rational and
philosophical principles." But this kind of critical
utterance is rarely associated with the subjective,
creative temperament. Tchaikovsky, with all his
reserve, cannot always hold up the mask of im-
personality between himself and his readers. Thus,
in what is often a dry record of musical events, we
come upon oases of purely personal appreciation.
And what positive good sense, what lucidity and
soberness of judgment, what liberal-minded eclecticism
we find in these pages! They are "appreciations"
in the intellectual rather than the emotional sense;
for Tchaikovsky—to borrow a phrase from Mr.
Hadow—never condescends to substitute mere auto-
biography for criticism. We who in England know
Tchaikovsky so well—so much too well—by his
Sixth Symphony, are disposed to interpret the whole
trend of his character by this one dark-toned work,
which may reflect—for all we know—as much the
tragic historical destinies of his country as the
shadow of a purely personal sorrow. This work
has now come to be regarded as the expression
of Tchaikovsky's creed—or want of creed; and,
according to the more or less morbid temperament

of its commentators, "The Pathetic" is made to represent him as something between a fallen angel weeping "ever through vasts forgotten of the sun," and a whimpering agnostic prig. For my part, I think we shall never appreciate the true greatness of Tchaikovsky until we have forgotten, for a time, the over-wrought emotion of the *Sixth Symphony* and the fascinating triviality of its musical antithesis, the *Casse-Noisette Suite.* Then perhaps we shall turn with pleasure to the wholesome vigour and dramatic interest of *The Tempest;* to the poetic sentiment, the intense passion, the poignant—but controlled — melancholy of *Francesca di Rimini,* one of the most beautiful examples of programme music ever written; and the numerous other interesting works of his best and most robust period. Meanwhile it is good to see Tchaikovsky in a sober, business-like capacity, sane and clear-headed, exercising his critical faculties with a discretion and reserve that goes far to correct any false impressions of his extreme morbid subjectivity.

Tchaikovsky's first musical article, a message of consolation and encouragement to Rimsky-Korsakov, appeared in the *Sovremennaya Lietopis* in 1868. It was not, however, until 1872 that, yielding to the pressure of circumstances, he resolved to add to his income by regular journalistic work. During the next four years he wrote for the Moscow papers; first for the *Sovremennaya Lietopis* and afterwards for the *Russky Vestnik.* In 1876, disgusted by the polemics which he considered had been unjustly fastened upon him, he resigned his post as musical critic. On the opening of the Bayreuth Theatre, however, he was induced to act once more as correspondent for the *Russky Vestnik*, and recorded in five long articles his impressions of the *Nibelungen Ring*. Twelve years later he again took up the pen and published, in a series of twelve articles, portions of a journal kept during his tour of 1888.

Tchaikovsky's journalistic work, says Laroche, "made no impression upon his subsequent development, and left hardly any visible trace upon his life." At the close of the sixties and during the seventies, Tchaikovsky's genius was abnormally active. One work after another took shape in his brain with a feverish and exhausting rapidity ; and to a man thus preoccupied by the things of the imagination the weekly letter to the *Russky Vestnik* was a tax. He was oppressed by an almost fateful realisation of the shortness of his working days. To him *ars longa, vita brevis*, was no mere copybook phrase. He was haunted with a fear lest he should "die with all his music in him," and more than once in his life he paid the penalty for his feverish activity in periods of enforced idleness and depression. The lust of finishing left its mark upon his work. "He wrote, wrote, wrote in haste," says Laroche, "using up bales of music paper ; not finishing his work at once, or rather—to be quite accurate—finishing it as regards externals, and conscientiously attending to technical details, but frequently in his eagerness losing sight of the plan and proportions of the whole." This accounts for the destruction of so many of his earlier works and the constant rewriting and modification of others.

The collected criticisms of Tchaikovsky must not be taken as more than a partial indication of his thoughts on music, for it will be evident that the concerts of the Musical Society at Moscow, and the performances at the Opera, gave only a limited field in which to express his views.

What, then, were Tchaikovsky's musical ideals in his youth and maturity, and how far did they influence his individual development? He himself would have repudiated the use of the word "ideals." He had the positive Russian temperament that feels intensely, and instinctively avoids gush. Was it not a Russian who remarked that a piece of bread and cheese was worth all the poems of Poushkin put together? In a similarly practical manner Tchaikovsky answered those who questioned him about his inner consciousness.

"What are your musical ideals?" Serov's daughter inquired of Tchaikovsky as he sat at the piano during one of her father's musical evenings in Petersburg.

"My ideals?" he answered: "is it absolutely necessary to have ideals in music? I have never given a thought to them." Then, after a few moments' reflection: "I never possessed any ideals."

To another lady who put the same question he replied: "My ideal is to become a good composer."

I

MOZART AND HAYDN

TCHAIKOVSKY, says Laroche, was constant in his leading ideas, but very variable in the shades of his opinion. The chief deity of his musical Olympus was Mozart. In this he differed from the majority of his countrymen, who, preferring fire to light, and intensity of emotion to "sweet reasonableness," have rarely appreciated Mozart at his immeasurable worth. Glinka thought *Don Juan* "a fine opera, but not a model one." Tchaikovsky writes of it :—

"Every work of art, however much it may transcend the artistic level of the day and the society in which its author lived and moved, must still inevitably bear the stamp of its period. No matter how strong and profound the creative gift of an artist, he cannot escape certain characteristics, certain purely external peculiarities of form which, in the hands of second-rate talent, degenerate into mere tricks of routine and finally assume a sort of archæological importance. Therefore it is not surprising that even in the loftiest spheres of art the works of human genius should grow obsolete. In the creations of Raphael, Shakespeare, and Mozart, despite all their depth of conception, we find certain external features which do not answer to the tastes of younger generations. But it does not follow that the hand of time has power to touch the essential substance of a work of art ; and so—notwithstanding its eighty years— the opera of *Don Juan*, in which are enshrined the powerful and incorruptible relics of Mozart's genius, is only old-fashioned as regards technical details. It awakes in us the same enthusiasm, it touches our feelings as effectively as in the days of our fathers and grandfathers before us. Compared with that of Berlioz, Mozart's orchestration is, of course, slight ; his arias are somewhat diffuse, and sometimes err by pandering to the caprices and virtuosity of his singers. His style is laid out to please the affectations of the court-circle of his day. Nevertheless, all his operas, and *Don Juan* above all, are full of beauties of the highest order and of strong dramatic situations. His melody is wonderfully beautiful, his harmony rich and interesting. But Mozart was pre-eminently a master of dramatic music, and no other composer ever created such well-sustained or realistically conceived musical types as Don Juan, Donna Anna, Leporello, Zerlina, etc.

" As I have remarked, Mozart's weak side lies in his lengthy concert arias, which, purposely designed that the singer might show off his or her skill, are not invariably of great musical value. But in the concerted parts, in the scenes which depict dramatic movement, he has left us a long series of masterpieces. The scenes in which Donna Anna takes part are especially strong in this intense dramatic power. Her heart-rending cries over the body of her murdered father, her horror and thirst for vengeance when she meets the author of her misfortunes, all this is realised by Mozart with such convincing power that its effect can only be compared with some of Shakespeare's best scenes.

"I would point out as the best things in the opera the *Finale* of the first act; the scene at the grave of the Commandant; the sextet in the second act (when the rest of the characters mistake Leporello for Don Juan), so remarkable for its humorous contrast to the rest of the work; and, finally, the last scene between Don Juan and the Statue.

"To what simple—I might almost say poor—means Mozart had recourse in this scene in order to express the horror of the impenitent libertine before this awful apparition! Contemporary composers would have let loose upon us the full tornado of trombones, trumpets, cymbals, and drums; whereas Mozart attains an infinitely stronger effect by the actual strength of his genius alone."

To this love for Mozart, Tchaikovsky remained faithful during his whole life. He studied the composer from every side of his genius, and left two memorials of his affection for him: his "Mozartiana" Suite for Orchestra (op. 61), and the vocal quartet

"Night," the music adapted from Mozart's *Fantasia* No. 4 (1893).

A few days before his death Tchaikovsky conducted the dances from *Idomeneo*. "His admiration for the composer of *The Magic Flute*," says Laroche, "extended in a certain degree to his whole period, and he was delighted with one of Sarti's operas." In his own opera *La Dame de Pique*, there is a scene which might almost pass for the work of a contemporary of Mozart. But it cannot be said that he paid his favourite the flattering homage of imitation. In spite of his consistent admiration for Mozart, Tchaikovsky's genius had nothing in common with him, and Laroche explains this attraction by the theory of "unlike to unlike."

For Haydn, Tchaikovsky had a sincere, if conventional respect, and a due sense of his importance in the historical development of music. He thought his music valuable for educational purposes, and declared that a Haydn quartet was preferable to many chamber works of the modern German school. In 1873 he writes :—

"I have a very high regard for the respectable and even *great* services rendered to music by this venerable man. Haydn has immortalised himself, if not by his inventive powers, at least by what he did towards perfecting those two ideal forms—the Symphony and the Sonata—afterwards carried to the utmost degree of beauty and finished workmanship by Mozart and Beethoven. Haydn is an indispensable link in the chain of symphonic music; without him

Mozart and Beethoven could hardly have existed ; at least the development of these two dominant figures in the world of music would have been very different. They would have sprung from a less cultivated soil, and must have met with greater obstacles to the growth of their genius. But without in any way detracting from Haydn's invaluable services, we cannot fail to see that his inspiration did not soar very high ; that he never got beyond the 'miniature' and the 'pretty,' and never once touches those secret heart-strings from which later composers have drawn such soul-stirring, deeply pathetic tunes. This is not a suitable place for entering into the historical conditions under which Haydn's genius was developed. Would he have shown more depth, more tragic force, more passion if he had been born at some other period ? Does not his music owe its artificial atmosphere of elegant coldness to the customs and surroundings in which he chanced to develop ? Is not this the reason why he has no power to move us deeply, to draw our tears or to carry us away by strong emotions ? May not this be the reason why he has survived from the last century with difficulty, through a period torn by doubt and exhausted by the irresponsible sufferings of the romantic school which followed him ? These deep and interesting questions may be discussed by lovers of musical æsthetics. I have said that Haydn belongs entirely to the sphere of the 'pretty' in art. In all his symphonies you may find the same playful episodes, a sort of medley, or kaleidoscopic play of sounds which involuntarily charms the ear. By this

I do not for a moment mean to suggest that Haydn should be irrevocably excluded from the concert-room. In Russia, especially, his works form a necessary stepping-stone by means of which we can lead on the mass of our public until it attains to the level of Beethoven and learns to appreciate him. Only it is desirable to contrast with his slightness and superficiality of form and idea some great work by one of the later masters."

II

TCHAIKOVSKY did not share the revived interest in Bach which made itself felt in Russia, as elsewhere, towards the middle and close of the fifties, and spoke of his great choral works as " real classical bores "; while Handel he found intolerable.

If his preference for Mozart, who is in many respects his musical antithesis, is somewhat unaccountable, so, at first sight, his want of sympathy for Chopin has its element of mystery. For many years he felt no enthusiasm whatsoever for the works of the Polish master, and would only grudgingly admit that there was a certain " charm " in the *Barcarolle* and the *F minor Fantasia*. Yet there is undoubtedly some affinity between Chopin and Tchaikovsky in temperament and, in a much less degree, in style. Both have the tendency to alternate between profound melancholy and fiery energy characteristic of the Slav; both have the same rather morbid preference for the minor, the same chromatic colouring; the same restless agitation in the middle parts. Tchaikovsky seems to have been aware of this likeness, and to have turned from Chopin as from a reflection of his own weaknesses. In later days, Nicholas Rubinstein partially converted Tchaikovsky from this prejudice against Chopin's works.

It is not easy to arrive at a clear view of Tchaikovsky's attitude towards Beethoven. "Generally speaking," says Laroche, "he cherished a sentiment of *veneration* for Beethoven, quite distinct from the enthusiastic *affection* and true worship which he felt for Mozart." There are indications in his articles that he sometimes resented the general tendency to an indiscriminate Beethoven worship. But Tchaikovsky is often so reserved in his writings, so averse from rashly running counter to opinions which have been consecrated by authority, that his views on Beethoven seem rather colourless. In conversation he was less reticent, but there seems always to have been an element of doubt as to his real feelings on this subject. "In 1867," writes Laroche, "I showed him a MS. (part of my article on Glinka) treating of the exaggerated fanaticism with which Beethoven was regarded. He then praised me for my manliness, in what certainly did not sound like empty phrases ; but when eighteen years later I developed the same idea in various articles, and at greater length, he showed himself very reserved, and merely remarked that I was unjust to the *Finale* of the *Ninth Symphony.*" Tchaikovsky started life as a great admirer of Glinka, and, like all young Russian composers, was proud of the independent views upon Western art which were part of the master's legacy to the school he had founded. Glinka certainly venerated Beethoven, but just as he shocked all cultivated Russia by his criticisms of Bellini and other Italian idols of his day, so his disciples went a step further and scandalised a later generation of formalists by repudiating their obligation to traditions which their nation had in no way helped to build up. It may have begun as a rebellion; it ended in the constitutional protest of a foreign-ridden people. Tchaikovsky was not a stranger to this movement; but a period of eighteen years works changes in a malleable nature. In his maturity he grew more eclectic, more tolerant of tradition; and it is easy to conceive that he mistrusted the two-edged blade of Laroche's criticism, which, while striking a blow at venerable traditions, was often equally hostile to the music of the New School. From numerous criticisms I have endeavoured to collect the passages about Beethoven in which the personal note seems to be of some value. In 1871 I find the following paragraph :—

"I am not disposed to proclaim the infallibility of Beethoven's principles, and, without in any way denying his historical importance, I protest against the insincerity of an equal and indiscriminate laudation of all his works. But undoubtedly in certain of his symphonies Beethoven reached a height to which scarcely any of his contemporaries could attain."

In the list of Beethoven's "unrivalled works" he places the *Eighth Symphony*, and a year after writing the above paragraph he drew the following comparison between the *Eighth* and the *Ninth Symphonies*, which is, I think, one of the most subjective of his criticisms :—

"Beethoven's *Eighth Symphony* is distinguished from its predecessors and from the one which followed it—the great *Choral Symphony*—by an unusual conciseness of form and by its unbroken joyfulness and festal character. It is the last bright smile, the last response given by the poet of human sorrow and hopeless despair to the voice of gladness. In the *Ninth Symphony* Beethoven concludes his colossal work by a Hymn to Joy, which represents the eternal and universal chorus of humanity, united in brotherly love and chanting in one voice an ecstatic dithyrambus to Nature and the Creator. But such joy is not of this earth. It is something ideal and unrealisable ; it has nothing in common with this life, but is only a momentary aspiration of humanity towards the holiness which exists only in the world of art and beauty ; afterwards, this vale of earth, with its endless sorrow, its agony of doubt and unsatisfied hopes, seems still more gloomy and without issue. In the *Ninth Symphony* we hear the despairing cry of a great genius who, having irrevocably lost faith in happiness, escapes for a time into the world of unrealisable hopes, into the realm of broken-winged ideals. The *Eighth Symphony*, on the contrary, is filled with a spirit of serene content and unrestrained joy. It depicts the gentle earthly delights of humanity, before the soul is distracted by evil, doubt, and despair.

"Both subjects of the first movement are full of grace and elegance, their exposition is simple and concise, with a delicate accompaniment and transparent harmony. The second subject is exceedingly original by reason of its unexpected modulations and capricious changes of tonality. The second movement (*Andante scherzando*) shares popular favour with the famous *Allegretto* of the *Seventh Symphony*. Its originality lies chiefly in the employment of the wind instruments which, contrary to the customary laws of instrumentation, are used by Beethoven as an accompaniment, while the violins keep up a lively —almost humorous—melody, and the basses reply heavily in a similar phrase. All this is unexpected, fresh, and piquant. The third movement, in the form and tempo of a minuet, recalls, by its style and by the unpretentious simplicity of its leading idea, the minuets of Haydn. In the *Finale*—one of Beethoven's symphonic *chefs-d'œuvre*—we meet with an endless series of humorous and unexpected episodes; of contrasts in harmony, varied modulations, and ingenious orchestral effects. I must indicate the striking unison effect of the whole orchestra on C♯, which breaks in so unexpectedly upon the remote key of C major, just after the *diminuendo* where Beethoven recalls the first subject in different registers of the various instruments; and again, the very humorous effect—twice repeated—which he gets by

the combination of drums and bassoons on the note
F, in succeeding octaves, struck at regular intervals,
staccato. The *Finale* abounds in such interesting
details."

His account of the *Seventh Symphony* seems also
worth quoting :—

"Beethoven's *Seventh Symphony*, thanks to its
well-known *Allegretto*,[1] is a great favourite with the
public. Among the works of the great symphonist,
this *Allegretto* plays something of the same part as
what is known as the *air favori* in a popular
opera. Very often such an air is only distinguished
from the numbers that precede or follow it because
the melody is more vulgar, the harmony coarser and
less poetical. To fine gradations of artistic colouring the majority is always blind. Bright tints, florid
outlines, and strong colouring—effects which catch
the eye—these alone can attract their attention.
Tender half-tones, finished details, elegant roundness
of form, all this escapes the notice of these unfortunate victims of blindness. A long time must
elapse before details, at first unobserved and mis-
understood, begin to detach themselves from the
background of the picture. The more a musical
work becomes the property of the public, the more
they begin to observe with astonishment all the
beauties they failed to appreciate at first hearing. At
the same time they grow disenchanted with their *air
favori*, discover that it is commonplace, and finally
turn it into the streets, where it becomes the property

[1] Tchaikovsky invariably speaks of this movement as an *Andante*.

of the grateful organ-grinder who caters for a public that never outgrows the *air favori*.

"But there exist some rare compositions which possess the power of pleasing alike the educated and uneducated public. Their beauty is immutable ; the oftener we hear them the more we love them. Their power and originality is such that it is impossible to analyse them ; but they can never become ephemeral because they are inaccessible to imitation and plagiarism. To this class of music belongs the *Allegretto* of the *Seventh Symphony*, which — for over sixty years—has been a fertile source of delight to the whole civilised world. The first and last movements of this wonderful work, which shine with the same radiance as when they astonished all Europe. in 1812—when Beethoven first took them from his portfolio—are not inferior to the *Allegretto*; but the latter, I repeat, has the privilege of popularity, thanks partly to its fascinating melody and partly to material beauty of sound—its admirable instrumentation.

"The first movement of the symphony opens with a broad, bold Introduction, and is remarkable for the gradual increase of interest with which Beethoven develops it, by means of what is known in technical terms as the 'elaboration' of a simple, short theme of an energetic character. The orchestral effect at the opening of this Introduction is very original, and is frequently repeated in that which follows. The whole mass of instruments give out loud staccato chords from which is formed the theme

of the Introduction, at first imperceptibly, but afterwards announced and sustained by the oboe.   The
first subject of the *Allegro*, a melody of a naïve,
pastoral character, served the purists of Beethoven's
day as a pretext for accusing him of a want of dis-
crimination in his choice of symphonic themes : as
though an artist who painted the sublime in Alpine
scenes or tempests at sea might not be equally
successful in representing a simple rural landscape.

"The rhythm of this theme, with its original
accent on the third beat of the bar, is maintained
with wonderful skill throughout the entire movement.[1]   Modulations, modifications of the themes,
strikingly new and bold harmonies, succeed each
other with ever-increasing interest, but the fundamental rhythm, which holds the first place, remains
unchanged throughout.   It is impossible to translate
into words the astounding effect of this infinite
variety in unity ; only a colossal genius such as
Beethoven could bring such a task to a successful
issue without wearying the attention of his audience,
or allowing them for a moment to feel anything
but pleasure in the importunate reiteration of the
first rhythmic figure.   Among other details of this
wonderful work I would point out the *stretto* at the
close of the first movement, where the bassi, 'celli,
and alti repeat twenty times in succession a little
two-bar phrase, while the higher registers of the
orchestra move in a progressive development of the

[1] I have printed this sentence as it appears in the Russian,
but I consider *third* evidently a misprint for *first*.

tonic-chord. This original method of procedure, like the inaugural chord of the Introduction, has served as a model for numerous imitators, among them Berlioz, who makes use of a similar effect at the end of the first movement of his *Romeo and Juliet* symphony.

"The *Allegretto* consists of the development of a rhythmic figure unusually simple in conception, and this simple leading idea lends to the movement that undeniable charm to which it owes its great popularity. This figure is first heard in the lower registers, from the alti, 'celli, and bassi. When it passes to the violins, it becomes associated in the 'celli with a sad, complaining phrase of contrapuntal character in the minor. Gradually the leading subject grows and becomes more and more prominent, until at last it is given out by the full power of the orchestra. Afterwards follows a contrasting melody, serene and joyful, suggestive of hope in some as yet remote happiness. Meanwhile the original rhythm, like a whispered foreboding, a gloomy *momento mori*, is heard in the bassi. When the leading subject returns, it is completely transformed, and receives its final development in a *fugato* form. Then it dies away, to reappear in a fragmentary way as though it still had something to say, and finally ceases altogether on a vague chord. If we, after all these years, are still astonished by the novelty and freshness, the power shown both in the design and execution of this marvellous work, what must our forefathers have felt when Beethoven by the magic power of his genius first raised the curtain which hid this ideal world of eternal beauty and harmony from human eyes?

" The *Scherzo* is full of life and joyous movement, and in the middle episode Beethoven gives it a character of triumphal, solemn joy.   In this movement occurs another striking and novel effect—exceedingly original for the period at which it was written—I refer to the pedal-point on the dominant, in contrast to the upper parts and the accent on the appoggiatura.

" If in contrast to the serious character of the *Allegretto* the *Scherzo* is remarkable for its joyful mood, the *Finale* is almost bacchanalian, and depicts a whole series of scenes replete with unconstrained gladness and contentment with life.   Hearing this superb last movement, we do not know which to admire most : the creative imagination of Beethoven, or the perfection of form, his astounding skill in handling all musical means, both in the development of the themes and in the fulness and luxuriance of his orchestration."

III

I HAVE said that in spite of his great love for Mozart, Tchaikovsky was not directly influenced by him, but as regards Schumann the case is completely reversed. In 1862 he was already a student of Schumann's works, and constantly played the symphonies and overtures arranged for four hands with his friend Laroche. Tchaikovsky's *opinion* of Schumann was variable, and rarely rose to whole-hearted approbation ; but Schumann's *influence* is traceable throughout the whole of his career, though gradually weakening as time progressed. One of his earliest criticisms of Schumann is that of the *Fourth Symphony*, in 1871 :—

"It may be said with truth that in the future history of the art the music of the second half of this century will be known to coming generations as 'Schumannesque.' Schumann's music, which is organically allied to Beethoven's, while at the same time sharply differentiated from it, reveals a whole

world of new musical forms, and touches heart-cords
which have never yet vibrated at the bidding of his
predecessors. In it we seem to catch an echo of
those profound, mysterious stirrings of our spiritual
life, of the doubt, the despair, the yearning towards
the Ideal, which agitate the hearts of the men and
women of to-day. History has not yet taken
cognisance of Schumann; only in the distant future
will it be possible to make an objective critical
evaluation of his work. But it is an undisputed
fact that this composer is the brightest star among
recent musicians; for hardly any good concert is
now given which does not include at least one of
Schumann's multitudinous works, in which his creative
power is proportionate to his wonderful productive-
ness.

"At a recent concert, given by the Musical
Society, we heard Schumann's *Fourth Symphony* (D
minor) and the little piece for piano, *Abends*,
which, in spite of its brevity, is full of charm and
true genius. I am even inclined to give the palm to
this exquisitely poetical trifle rather than to the
greater symphonic work. The *Fourth Symphony* is
the last[1] of the series, and at the same time the
least in value. It has not that overwhelming power,
that searching pathos, which strikes us in the first
two symphonies. The sum-total of its beauties cannot unfortunately redeem that great fault which prevails in all works of Schumann, considered especially

[1] It is really the second in order of production, a fact which
Tchaikovsky seems to have overlooked.

as a symphonic writer. This fault would be called by painters a lack of colour; it is a pallor, a dryness — I may almost say harshness — of orchestration. Without entering into technical details, I may explain to my readers that the art of instrumentation (*i.e.* the distribution of a work among the various instruments) consists in understanding how to employ alternately the individual groups of instruments; how to blend them appropriately; how to economise strong effects, and also in the intelligent use of colouring—that is to say, the application of *timbre* to musical ideas. This knowledge Schumann has not acquired. His orchestra works continuously; all the instruments take part in the exposition and development of his ideas. They are not used in detachments; there is no contrast between them (and contrasting effects are inexhaustible in orchestration); most of the time they mingle in a continuous roar, often spoiling the best parts of the work. As regards instrumentation, Schumann not only stands on a lower level than such masters as Berlioz, Mendelssohn, Meyerbeer, and Wagner, but he cannot even be compared with many second-rate composers who have borrowed his best inspirations."

Tchaikovsky regards Schumann's *Second* and *Third Symphonies* as the culminating points of his orchestral work; especially the *Second*, in which "the depth of thought, beauty of form, and breadth of plastic conception take us by surprise." But it is to the *First Symphony* that he has devoted the longest and most careful analysis, and for which he seems to feel a warm personal appreciation, which does not, however, disarm his critical attitude. Writing in the *Russky Viedomosti* in 1872, he says :—"Schumann's *First Symphony* was written in 1841, and was his earliest attempt in that species of composition. Beginning to compose at twenty, and having produced a number of fine pianoforte works and a quantity of songs, Schumann waited until his thirty-first year to approach orchestral music. The very fact that this master took up symphonic music so late seems to prove that he had no strong inclination towards the orchestra. A great connoisseur of all the qualities and most subtile resources of his favourite instrument —the piano—he is an inimitable master in the art of drawing out the rich, luxuriant sonority of this miniature orchestra. But apparently Schumann could never call forth the inexhaustible treasures of the modern orchestra. All his later works reveal his lack of a sense of colour, of genial design. He disdained colour, and preferred the pen and pencil to the brush. The most enthusiastic admirers of Schumann's music—which is invariably rich in invention and pale in colouration—are agreed that his orchestral works actually gain in being transcribed for the piano. Schumann had not the art of clothing his wealth of ideas in beautiful sounds; his orchestration is always opaque and heavy, and lacks brilliance and transparency. This characteristic negative feature of Schumann's genius is not often present in his *First Symphony*. It is said that he wrote this work under the strong influence and personal guidance of

Mendelssohn. The traces of this influence are not, however, apparent. Schumann, in his *First Symphony*, with all its positive and negative qualities, shows more strength and capability and greater individuality than Mendelssohn. On the one hand, wealth of imagination, simplicity of design, the plasticity of a Beethoven in its fundamental form ; on the other, a lack of colour, obscurity, and a disregard of attractive details in orchestration—this is what we find in Schumann's first essay in symphonic writing.

" The work opens with an Introduction in which the leading idea is announced in a slow *tempo* by a few of the brass instruments and is repeated by the whole orchestra. This is, as it were, the signal which heralds the sumptuous, motley pageant which unfolds itself as the work proceeds. The triumphant joy of the first subject gives place to an episode of a contrasting character which—in spite of all contrast —has a close connection with that which precedes it. It is evident that these are twin themes and originated simultaneously in Schumann's mind ; their union is not marred by that unsightly join which always shows in the works of inferior composers with their superficial habit of pasting their thoughts together. In working out this subject, Schumann, without departing from classical forms, as laid down by Mozart and Beethoven, introduces entirely new methods of procedure, and displays an independence completely free from the influence of the earlier masters. The whole of this first movement proves that new, romantic, and original ideas can be united to the established traditions of form ; it is, as it were, the link which connects the classical school, ending with Beethoven, to the new movement in which Schumann joined with Chopin and Berlioz. The rest of the symphony bears also the stamp of this eclecticism. In the *Andante*, a beautiful melody of an elegiac character, accompanied by brilliant variations, produces a fascinating effect, especially when it passes to the 'celli in the key of the subdominant. In the third movement, the rhythm of which recalls a minuet rather than a scherzo such as we find in Beethoven's symphonies, the first trio is specially remarkable for the ingenious chords which seem to call to each other alternately from the string and wind instruments, and also for its concluding coda with its rushing syncopated rhythm and highly original harmony. The *Finale*, bold, brilliant, and finished in form, rich in beautiful modulations and in varied rhythm and harmony, serves as an admirable close to this exquisite work."

Another interesting example of Tchaikovsky's views upon Schumann is the following account of the *Pianoforte Quintet* (op. 44) :—

" It is a fact that Schumann, with his colossal creative gifts, yet lacked the particular instinct which might have enabled him to express his thoughts through the medium of orchestral or chamber music. In this he resembled Chopin, the pianist composer *par excellence*. . . . In spite of the luxuriant beauty scattered throughout his symphonic works, as regards form, structure, and finish, the first place must be given to Schumann's purely pianoforte works and to the chamber music in which the piano plays the chief part. To this class belongs the fine *Quintet in E flat*.

"The first movement is based on two very simple but striking and beautiful subjects, of contrasting character. The *Andante*, in the style and rhythm of a funeral march, depicts on a small scale a whole sombre tragedy. After the exposition of the wonderful leading subject, Schumann passes on to tributary ideas which have a solemn religious colouring, and seem to express faith and self-renunciation, a gentle submission to Providence, and a willingness to bow before the inevitable decrees of Fate. Then the gloomy theme of the funeral march returns, to be suddenly interrupted by a stormy episode which echoes the voice of a passionate soul agitated and rebellious at the tragic loss of some beloved being. But the notes of the funeral march break once more upon this music, like the lamentations of a broken heart. Gradually, a tender religious sentiment conquers all other emotions; the agitated spirit grows calm, and strives to become reconciled to the oppression of earthly life by looking forward to the beauty of heaven. The *Andante* comes to an ethereal close on the transparent major tonic chord, given out in harmonics by violins and viola in their highest flute-like register. The *Scherzo* is full of virile energy and inspired impetuosity. The *Finale* carries the listener back to the joyous mood of the first movement; and here, by starting the leading subjects of the first and last movements on 'pedal-points,' Schumann displays his inimitable technical skill in the polyphonic development of his themes. This is one of the inexplicable musical phenomena of genius before which musical specialists can only bow down in respect."

In his youth Tchaikovsky was a devotee of Italian opera, especially of Rossini's more serious works, *Semiramide*, *Otello*, and *Tell*. His appreciation of the *Barber of Seville* was of later growth. Tchaikovsky, though rarely stooping to direct imitation, was extremely susceptible to external influences. Italian opera was, moreover, associated in his case with a love episode which—though ephemeral in character—left a lingering sentimental impression in his memory. For Donizetti he felt no sympathy, but comparatively late in life—when the current of fashion had set in quite other directions—Tchaikovsky began to value the works of Bellini. But it was the glamour and warmth of the South, so forcibly expressed by Rossini's brilliant dramatic power, which exercised the strongest fascination for the Russian composer. He shared with the Italian school the cult of graceful and sensuous melody, and was strongly influenced by Rossini in this respect. We cannot doubt it, when we recall, for instance, some of the solos in his opera *The Oprichnik*, or the second subject of the first movement of the *Sixth Symphony*. The lovely things of art are preserved to reappear in unexpected disguises, and just as the gracious beauty of Italian melody seemed doomed to pass away under a new dispensation, it was reincarnated in the works of this northern composer. Such cases of musical atavism are by no means rare, and would make an interesting study in themselves.   Tchaikovsky's views on Italian music, written at a time when all critics who wished to be taken seriously were condemning Italian opera, in the words of Dr. Johnson, as "an exotic and irrational entertainment," were admirable in their tone of unbiassed reserve.   His attitude was that of negative rather than of positive defence.   He refused to exalt Wagner and Schumann at the expense of Rossini and Meyerbeer, and succeeds in keeping an open mind and an individual opinion throughout the period of heated polemics during which he acted as a musical critic.

The note of decision which is sometimes lacking in Tchaikovsky's defence of Italian opera is fully heard, however, on the question of classical music, in the narrower sense of the word—that is to say, the great period at the close of the eighteenth and beginning of the nineteenth centuries.   While he gives Schumann one of the highest places in modern music, he scarcely veils his contempt for the rank and file of the new romantic school of Germany.   Nor could he bring himself—even after conscientious efforts— to accept Brahms as one of the Immortals.   In the seventies, the period during which Tchaikovsky was engaged in musical criticism, Brahms's works were so seldom given in Moscow that his name rarely appears in the first part of this volume.   The first important record of Tchaikovsky's opinion on this subject occurs in November 1872, when Brahms's *Sextet in B flat* was given at one of the chamber concerts of the Musical Society. He then writes :—

"All Germany has looked with unction upon this composer,—who is still young,—thinking to find in him the man destined to lead his art into unexplored paths, and capable, by the power of his creative gift, not only of equalling, but even of surpassing, his great predecessors. The rumours circulated throughout the German musical world on the appearance of Brahms's first compositions owed their origin to Schumann. It is a well-known fact that great composers are rarely endowed with infallible critical instincts, and are generally remarkable for their leniency to their fellow-artists. Schumann is a striking example of this critical indulgence. All his life he bowed down to Mendelssohn, Chopin, and Berlioz, and even to such musical nobodies as Henselt, Hiller, etc. He went into sincere ecstasies over every fresh manifestation of genius, and only depreciated his own value. Towards the end of his career, Schumann, through the medium of his musical journal, published in Leipzig, began to prophesy the advent of a musical Messiah, who was destined to illuminate the whole world of music and to fill the place left vacant by Beethoven. When Brahms's first sonatas appeared, Schumann, in one laconic phrase, 'He has come,' announced the advent of the expected genius, whom he proclaimed in the person of young Brahms. Time has proved, however, that Schumann's unexpected proclamation was a mistake into which the indulgent and amiable

composer was easily led. Brahms has not fulfilled
the obligations which Schumann laid upon him and
upon all musical Germany personified in him. He
is merely one of those *routinier* composers in which
the German school has been so rich. He writes
fluently, skilfully, correctly, but without a spark of
independent genius ; contenting himself with endless
trifling with empty musical ideas, long since become
stale, and borrowed chiefly from Mendelssohn ; while
he also strives to imitate certain external mannerisms
of Schumann's. Brahms, however, is not devoid of
talent ; therefore he stands a whole head above his
contemporaries. But there is now no question of
the fulfilment of impossible hopes in his genius."

Sixteen years later Tchaikovsky's views upon
Brahms were less crude, and tempered by a sentiment
of personal respect, but they remained essentially
unchanged. During this period he had more
frequent opportunities of hearing the works of the
German master, and Kashkin says that during the
long, quiet evenings of Tchaikovsky's life at Klin,
he would often take one of Brahms's scores from his
shelves and try to work himself up to a flickering
enthusiasm for the contents. But there is no doubt
that these two great musicians found no common
meeting-ground, and Brahms on his part was too
sincere to pretend to any appreciation of Tchaikovsky's works. The unsympathetic attitude of the
Russian composer towards Brahms's music is regarded by many in the light of a grievance, or even
of an impertinence. Is it not really a blessing in

disguise? An artist may admire his great predecessors to the extent of being influenced by them, but no more; whereas a whole-hearted admiration for a contemporary seems invariably to lead to more or less direct imitation of his methods. The Brahms cult has immolated too many rising talents as it is; for even those who have the most genuine admiration for the splendid qualities of the master cannot deny that his disciples form the dullest school in contemporary music. In the independence of the Russian school—with its many imperfections—there is at least the charm of freshness and sincerity.

IV

COLD as was Tchaikovsky's attitude to Wagner's music in his early days, it is somewhat singular to find that the works of the Arch-Wagnerian Serov moved him to enthusiastic praise. *Judith*[1] was one of his favourite operas, and remained so through his whole life. But Serov left no traces of influence upon Tchaikovsky's own works, which show a close acquaintance with the dramatic compositions of Glinka and Meyerbeer, and later of Bizet and the modern French school. In connection with this school it may be said that, at first, Tchaikovsky was very little impressed by Gounod's *Faust*, which achieved such immense success in Petersburg. At a later date his favourite singer, Madame Artot, in the part of Margaret, partially dispelled this indifference. He had a great admiration for the orchestration of Berlioz, but he was not influenced

[1] *Judith*, an early opera of Serov's, was written in 1862, and performed in Petersburg in May 1863.

by him in the same degree as many of his compatriots : Moussorgsky, for instance, as regards sentiment, and Rimsky-Korsakov as regards style and technique. In March 1873, on the occasion of a performance of the overture to *Les Francs Juges*, he gives his opinion of Berlioz at considerable length :—

"Berlioz is both a brilliant and exceptional phenomenon in the history of music. In certain spheres of his art he has reached ideal heights to which few other artists have ever attained. He has not composed a single work which does not equally display all-round technical perfection and depth of thought, joined to beauty of form, which are essential properties of all great works of art. In many respects he has struck out in new lines, yet it cannot be said that he actually belongs to the new school ; nor has he left any direct disciples. Throughout his career he aroused great interest, but never possessed such warm partisans and patrons of his music as Mozart or Beethoven did, and—in our day —Wagner. The enthusiastic welcome accorded to him almost everywhere in Germany—with the exception of the stubborn attitude of the Leipzig Conservatoire—and also in Russia, was due not so much to a universal sympathy for his music as to certain side impulses. Germany and Russia honoured in the person of Berlioz his disinterested labours, his passionate love of art, his energetic and noble efforts to fight against the obtuseness, conventionality, ignorance, and intrigue of that brutal collection of units which poets call 'the crowd.' No matter how remarkable some sides of Berlioz's genius may be, no matter how prominently his sympathetic personality may stand out among the great musicians of our time, I still maintain that his music has never touched the masses in the same sense as that of Mozart, Beethoven, Schumann, Schubert, Mendelssohn, or Meyerbeer, or as that of Wagner must assuredly do in the future. That Berlioz was the victim of the misunderstanding of the French nation, led on by French musicians ; that he was never appreciated in that country ; that he was worthy of a better and happier fate than that which commonly falls to the lot of a persevering, hard-working artist— all this cannot be denied. But his isolated position among his contemporaries in art, his want of success, the coldness of the public and of musicians, these things are due to certain peculiarities of his exceptional musical temperament, and the incompleteness, in many respects, of his natural creative endowment.

" In composition we must distinguish two separate factors : a purely inventive faculty, and imagination. The history of music furnishes examples of composers who have possessed astonishing powers of the first order ; their minds have been inexhaustibly productive of beautiful melodic ideas and exquisite harmonies, which were not the outcome of any effort or labour, but of inherent instinct and tendency. But they lacked a rich, luminous imagination. In this connection we may instance Schubert, Chopin to a certain extent, and our Russian composer

Dargomijsky. Other composers, endowed with the second factor of the creative mind, but possessing relatively poor inventive faculties, know how to extract all the contents of a musical germ ; and by variety in the contrasts of colour, and by special attention to external beauty, they make the most of the situation. Such are Mendelssohn, Liszt, and Balakirev. An equal proportion of inventive power in melody, rhythm, and harmony, joined to wealth of imagination, is only to be found in the wake of the very greatest masters, such as Mozart and Beethoven. As regards Berlioz, he belongs undoubtedly to the second category of composers. The preponderance of fiery poetical imagination over absolute musical creative power is all the more apparent in him, because he is entirely lacking in the art of harmony, which is so indispensable to the development of leading ideas. His harmony is distorted, and sometimes intolerable to a finely organised ear. We hear in it an insane incoherence, the absence of any natural feeling, and an inconsequence in the management of the parts which prevents his works from appealing directly to the musical emotions of his audience. Berlioz works upon the imagination. He knows how to engage and interest ; but he can rarely move us. Poor in melodic inspiration, lacking a fine feeling for harmony, but endowed with a marvellous gift of exciting the imagination of his hearers, Berlioz applied all his creative powers to the externals of musical beauty. The results of this tendency are shown in that marvellous orchestration, that inimitable beauty of sonority, that picturesque musical presentment of the natural and fantastic world, which proclaim him the subtle and inspired poet, the unapproachably great master. We recall all the poetic glamour with which he depicts the supernatural world in his *Faust*, or the tiny fairy-folk in the scherzo 'Queen Mab,' from the *Romeo and Juliet* symphony. Here the music gives such a realistic picture of a fantastic subject that the imagination is carried away, as in a beautiful dream, to the unknown region where lies the valley of eternal and ideal happiness."

Tchaikovsky had a great respect for Monsieur Saint-Saëns as an all-round artist who combines a remarkable creative gift with refined and brilliant executive power. In 1875 the French musician visited St. Petersburg in the threefold capacity of composer, pianist, and conductor. In November he played his *Pianoforte Concerto in D flat* at a concert of the Musical Society, and Tchaikovsky then writes of him : " Monsieur Saint-Saëns belongs in his own country to a small circle which represents the progressive element in music. In this advanced set, which consists of the most talented of contemporary French composers—Massenet, Dubois, and Paladihle (also Bizet, a composer of extraordinary endowments who died last year at thirty years of age)—Monsieur Saint-Saëns occupies a very prominent position." He then gives a brief biographical sketch of the composer, and goes on to speak of the general features of his work : " All the most sympathetic characteristics of his nationality, cordial sincerity, warmth of feeling, intellect, make themselves felt in every note of our guest's compositions. They are further illuminated by his artistic interpretation of them, which shows such distinction, such thoughtful and careful phrasing, without a trace of affectation." Elsewhere, he dwells upon the union of strictly classical methods with modern sentiments which is so characteristic of Saint-Saëns. " If I am not mistaken," he says, " the originality of the French master's creative methods lies in the fact that he combines most successfully the style of Sebastian Bach—for whom he has an evident affection—with the national French elements, of which the characteristically piquant rhythm makes itself clearly felt."

As regards Wagner, it may be said that his influence is not at all evident in Tchaikovsky's early works, and only to a very limited extent in those of his maturity. Laroche, however, considers that Wagner's influence had perceptibly increased during the last years of Tchaikovsky's life, though more in the direction of technique than of sentiment. In 1862, all that Tchaikovsky knew of Wagner's music were the selections given at the concerts of the Russian Musical Society, and by Strauss at the Pavlovsky. " It might be supposed," says Laroche, " that the impressionable young composer would have fallen under Wagner's influence after the Easter concerts of 1863. But it was not so. Even the prelude to *Lohengrin*, which excited so much enthusiasm in the public, especially among the

students of the Conservatoire, was received by
Tchaikovsky in a cold, sceptical spirit."

His early views of Wagner are set forth in a
criticism of the *Faust Overture*, written in 1872.
"At the present moment," he writes, "Wagner is
undoubtedly the most striking personality on the
horizon of the musical world. His works are still
far from being understood by the general public,
either in Germany or abroad; nevertheless, by means
of his rabid polemic against all constituted authority
and by the vastness of the problems he has set himself to solve, he has succeeded in attracting to himself
the attention of the whole musical world, and even
in arousing the interest of those to whom music is
not a matter of everyday life. Some regard Wagner
as a musical light, second only to Beethoven; to
others he appears a charlatan in the style of our
'Abyssinian maestro'; but in any case, if we may
believe—not without justification—that Wagner
desired to win celebrity at any price, his aim is now
attained. He has ardent worshippers and equally
furious enemies who make it their business to write
about all his utterances, and his words are awaited in
a spirit of admiration, antagonism, or simple curiosity,
by the public of both hemispheres.

"Among those who labour at art or science we
may clearly distinguish two types. The one consists
of those who, in obedience to their vocation, select
the path which seems best suited to their powers and
most in conformity with their idiosyncrasies and lot
in life. They do not adopt any fashionable idea as

their device. They do not seek to clear their road by overthrowing authority ; nor do they constitute themselves the instruments of Providence whose duty it is to open the eyes of blind humanity. They labour, study, observe, and perfect themselves ; then they create, by virtue of their natural qualities and the circumstances of time and place in which they have developed. They work out their own problem, and, quitting the arena of life, leave the fruits of their labour for the pleasure and profit of future generations. To this type of 'artist-workers' belong Bach, Haydn, Mozart, Beethoven, Mendelssohn, Schumann, Glinka. Others, consumed by un-measured ambition, in order to attain more rapidly to a prominent position, push noisily through the crowd, dispersing right and left all whom they meet on their road, and striving to attract universal attention to themselves. Such artists are ready to pose as the representatives of every new—and sometimes false—idea, and strive, not for the realisation of their genius, but only to astonish the world by their Don Quixot-ism. To this type belong Wagner and Serov."

Wagner's personal vanity and chauvinistic tactics were hateful to the "Hermit of Klin." Moreover, Tchaikovsky—at least during the earlier years of his career—sincerely believed that Wagner was a sym-phonist *manqué*. An intimate friend of Wagner's once repeated to Tchaikovsky a remark which the com-poser of *Parsifal* had made to him in a moment of friendly conversation : " Even if I had desired to occupy myself with the composition of chamber music and symphonies it would have been impossible, since my duty lies within the limits of opera." "Do not these words of Wagner's"—comments Tchaikovsky—"show to what a degree a preconceived theory prejudiced the mind of this obstinate, richly-endowed, but narrow-minded German?"

His views were practically unchanged when, four years later, in 1876, he went to hear the *Nibelungen Ring* at Bayreuth. Laroche, who was also there in the capacity of musical critic, says that Tchaikovsky did not conceal from him the fact that the *Ring* did not afford him any pleasure. "But," adds Laroche, "the company among which he found himself at Bayreuth made it exceedingly difficult to say anything against Wagner. He had as an inseparable companion one of the professors of the Moscow University, Klindworth, who united an 'adoration' for Tchaikovsky with Wagnerism of the first water and of a most rabid description. In our hearts we Moscovites were all a little afraid of Klindworth, but Peter Ilich was particularly in awe of him, for he was by nature far more deferential and gentle than courageous." The result was that before others Tchaikovsky was either silent about Wagner's music or only spoke in praise of those particular features which happened to please him. But though both in 1863 and 1876 Tchaikovsky passed unmoved through these Wagnerian experiences, there came a moment when he was carried away by a sudden enthusiasm. This was in 1886, when he first saw the pianoforte score of *Parsifal*, and was delighted with the close of the last scene of the first act. From that time Laroche thinks that he began to look upon Wagner with different eyes, although he still kept to the laws of opera as formulated by Gluck, and was never attracted by the innovations of the Music Drama.

RUSSIAN MUSIC—GLINKA—DARGOMIJSKY

In order to understand Tchaikovsky's attitude towards the composers of his native land, it is necessary to know something of the rival schools of criticism which have divided musical opinion in Russia from the time of Glinka to the present hour. The chief Russian critics were at first unanimous in recognising in Glinka not only the leader of a national movement, but a composer worthy to be ranked with the great composers of all time. It was not until the appearance of his second opera, *Russlan and Ludmilla*, that the schism arose which led to endless controversy and extreme bitterness on the part of the representatives of both sides. On the one hand was Serov, who, taking his stand upon the Wagnerism principle "Opera must be music drama," endeavoured, in a series of articles entitled "Russlan and the Russlanists," to prove that whatever might be the intrinsic value of the work as regards music, it could not claim to be considered an opera. "*Russlan*," argues Serov, "has no dramatic interest ; its libretto is a thing of shreds and patches. It lacks historical significance, vitality, and the savour of real life. *A Life for the Tsar*, despite the literary weakness of its book, teems with human interest and has a definite dramatic development ; therefore it is legitimate opera. But *Russlan*, at the best, can only be considered as a series of delightful musical illustrations to fantastic scenes ; at the worst, as the interesting failure of a great, but wrong-headed, composer." On the opposite side we find an equally capable and fervent advocate in the person of M. Vladimir Stassov, the friend and biographer of Glinka. He is prepared to maintain that Glinka shows far greater creative power in *Russlan* than in his earlier works. He has thrown off the fetters of conventionality that impeded the free play of his genius in *A Life for the Tsar*, and reveals himself in his full maturity. *Russlan*, he thinks, must not be considered as an aberration of wilful genius, but as the deliberate work of a man who knows quite well the goal for which he is striving, but prefers to reach it by paths of his own.

A precisely similar difference of opinion exists with regard to the two great operas of Glinka's contemporary, Dargomijsky. His earlier effort, the fantastic opera of *The Russalka* (*Water Sprite*), was generally accepted as a work of great merit ; while the critics split upon the subject of *The Stone Guest*, some regarding it as the logical outcome of his artistic theories, and others as the last eccentricity of a warped and incoherent imagination.

Tchaikovsky had not the vigorous critical "mailed-fist" of Serov, nor his obstinate dogmatism and blind adherence to the Wagnerian creed. Neither had he the generous, comprehensive sympathy, nor the fine literary gift of Stassov. His views of Russian music were on the whole slightly coloured by those of Serov, but his remarks upon his compatriots have, generally speaking, a characteristic note of reserve which naturally failed to satisfy the leaders of either party. Writing about these differences of opinion, he says :—

"It is impossible not to see that Serov's criticism is the more rational. Looking at the question from a specific musical point of view, he never denies the merits of *Russlan* as regards musical material, or, indeed, any of its best qualities. But it is a well-known fact that great works of art are valued less for the undoubted creative force of their authors than for the perfection of form into which this force is moulded, and also for their symmetry and for the successful fusion of the idea and its external expression. Is not this the reason why Beethoven is considered the first of composers, although every musician knows that Mozart, and even Schubert, possessed as great—if not a greater—volume of musical inspiration? If we wished to indicate Glinka's place in the pantheon of musicians, for sheer strength of creative genius, we might place him among the greatest representatives of his art. But it is a fact that fate did not set Glinka in such an environment as was necessary to the full development of his gift. He was a lion in the sheepskin of dilettantism. . . . Like the rich young man in the parable, he possessed a fund of power which he did not realise, and never understood how to give it the direction it deserved. Although the character of his musical nature was pre-eminently lyric and symphonic, Glinka has left hardly any purely symphonic works. Yet, judging from certain episodes in his operas, he might have given us inimitable examples in this style. Deprived of a highly-cultured musical environment, and not having found the support he deserved, Glinka sought an outlet for his inspiration, and was carried away by the first subject that presented itself. He embraced it with ardour, never pausing to consider if it was suitable for a successful and serious work of art. For instance, *A Life for the Tsar* shows that Glinka was fascinated in this way by the contrasting effects of the mazurka-rhythm and the melancholy of the Russian songs. *Russlan* was written for the sake of a few fantastic scenes which had actually excited his musical inspiration — his *symphonic* rather than his *dramatic* instincts. Thus it follows that *A Life for the Tsar*, composed to an accidentally successful plot, turned out a fine opera ; while *Russlan*, consisting of disconnected fantastic scenes, put together at different times by different people, cannot be considered a model opera, because of its inorganic structure and total lack of dramatic interest. It is a fairy spectacle joined to most distinguished music."

Here we have a fairly clear statement of Tchai-

kovsky's opinion of Glinka as an operatic composer.
It is my immediate design merely to show Tchaikovsky as a musical critic, and not to discuss or
refute his opinions. But because our whole view of
Russian music will be true, or distorted, according to
our judgment of Glinka as the source from which it
flowed, it seems only just to say that—viewed in the
light of biographical facts—this idea of Glinka, as a
gifted but irresponsible amateur, requires considerable
modification. It is true that he was denied the
doubtful blessing of academic training, but when we
remember his sojourn in Italy, his visit to Paris,
where he listened to and learned from the music of
Berlioz, his musical tour in Spain, and his brief but
severe course of study under one of the first theorists
of his day, it is absurd to imagine that he entered
upon his operatic tasks with less preparation than the
average Conservatoire student. Can we believe that
Glinka, who for thirty years had meditated the
creation of a national opera, was induced to compose
A Life for the Tsar merely for the sake of contrasting
Russian and Polish rhythms? Equally the whole
history of his musical development contradicts the
theory that *Russlan* owes its existence to purely
fortuitous circumstances.

As Tchaikovsky looks upon Glinka as a great
symphonic composer, led astray by the tastes of the
society in which he lived, it is interesting to read
what he has to say about his finest effort in this
sphere of art. The incidental music to the tragedy
Prince Kholmsky is a most remarkable work, and

contains, besides the instrumental entr'actes, at least two of Glinka's finest songs.   But the work has never been appreciated by the Russian public, and is still unaccountably neglected in this country, where Russian music is often better received than it is in Petersburg and Moscow.   "In this composition," says Tchaikovsky, "Glinka shows himself one of the greatest symphonic composers of his day.   Many touches in *Prince Kholmsky* recall the brush of Beethoven.   There is the same moderation in the means employed and total absence of all striving after mere external effects ; the same sober beauty and clear exposition of ideas that are not laboured, but inspired ; the same plasticity of form and mould.   Finally, there is the same inimitable instrumentation, so remote from all that is affected or far-fetched ; strong, but never noisy ; solid, and free from all flimsiness or vagueness of harmonic design.   Every entr'acte which follows the overture is a little picture, drawn by a master-hand. They are symphonic marvels which would suffice a second-rate composer for a whole series of long symphonies."

Tchaikovsky has not much insight into the character of Dargomijsky's genius.   He himself was so invariably preoccupied with the purely musical beauty of his vocal works that he frequently sacrifices truth of expression to a love of graceful *cantilena*.   How then should he be in sympathy with Dargomijsky, to whom expressive realism was the chief aim of vocal art, and a fine literary text an object of veneration ?

He admits that *The Russalka*, by reason of its melodic charm, sincerity of inspiration, and elegance of *cantilena* and recitative, must be ranked next to the operas of Glinka. But he does not believe in his further development. The same unfavourable circumstances—the lack of academic training—which impeded the artistic evolution of Glinka, were, according to Tchaikovsky, equally prejudicial to Dargomijsky's career. He says : " It was only by means of his surprisingly delicate instinct, and his strong individuality, that Dargomijsky managed to attain, in certain aspects of opera, to a degree of perfection reached by only a few of the elect. His strength lay exclusively in his wonderful realism and in his eminently vocal recitative ; qualities which lend to his splendid opera the charm of inimitable originality. The composer recognised the dominant quality of his gift ; but this knowledge, which unfortunately was not supported by a sober, critical instinct, led him to the strange notion of composing an opera consisting entirely of recitative. With this intention, Dargomijsky selected the text of 'The Stone Guest' by Poushkin, and without altering a single letter of it, without adapting it to the practical demands of opera —he fitted recitative to every line of the lengthy text. We know that recitative has no definite rhythm, no clearly defined melody or musical form— it is merely the cement which unites the various parts of a musical edifice. It is indispensable, on the one hand, because of the ordinary conditions of scenic development ; and on the other, because it forms a contrast to the lyrical situations in the opera. What an aberration of a daring mind, unguided by any sober conception of æsthetic development! To write an opera without music—is not this the same as writing a drama without words or action?"

ALTHOUGH Tchaikovsky was sometimes influenced by Serov as a critic, and was entirely carried away by his enthusiasm for his early opera *Judith*, yet he was able to gauge with perfect accuracy the artificial causes of this composer's success. Writing of one of his later works, *Rogneda*, he says : " The continued success of this opera, and the firm place it has won in the Russian repertory, is due not so much to its intrinsic beauty as to the subtle calculation of effects which guided its composer. Beginning to write at a time of life when other and more strongly gifted composers are already on the wane, he worked less from inward impulse than because, having for years made a critical study of music in all its branches, he saw that he could take up the work rapidly and with ease. Undoubtedly a talented musician of such remarkable intellect, and possessed of such stores of varied erudition as Serov, had every chance of winning popular sympathy. The public of all nations are not particularly exacting in matters of æsthetics; they delight in external and sensational effects and violent contrasts, and are quite indifferent to deep and original works of art if their *mise en scène* are not highly coloured, showy, and brilliant. Thus it was with Serov. He knew how to catch the public; and if his opera suffers from poverty of melodic inspiration, from want of organic sequence, from weak recitative and declamation, and from harmony and instrumentation which are crude and merely decorative in effect—yet what sensational effects the composer succeeds in piling up! Mummers who turn into geese and bears, real horses and dogs, the touching episode of Ruald's death, the Prince's dream made actually visible to our eyes, the Chinese gongs made very audible to our ears, all this—the outcome of a recognised poverty of inspiration—literally crackles with startling effects. Serov, as I have said, had only a mediocre gift, united to great experience, remarkable intellect, and extensive erudition; therefore it is not surprising to find in *Rogneda* numbers—like rare oases in a desert—in which the music is excellent. Such are the Chorus of Idolaters in the second act; Iziaslav's charming little song: Rogneda's ballad; and the fine hymn with which the opera winds up. As to those numbers which are the special favourites of the public, as is so frequently the case, their real value proves to be in inverse proportion to the success they have won. For instance, the duet between Ruald and the Traveller is neither better nor worse than a dozen Italian operatic duets. The celebrated third act owes its success, on the one hand, to the beautiful chorus *à capella*, and, on the other, to the touching sentiment of faith and love—in the Christian sense of the word —which is awakened by the episode of Ruald's death."

With those members of the Russian school who were his more immediate contemporaries Tchaikovsky was rarely in complete sympathy. Naturally he could never be in touch with the talent of Moussorgsky, the fervent disciple of Dargomijsky's later doctrines of realism and declamatory science. For Balakirev he seems to have felt the respect due from one great craftsman to another. Here, at least, there could be no question of faulty training or amateur pretensions. He admired Balakirev as a conductor, and regretted that his counsels of perfection led to such a small output as regards composition.

I have mentioned that his first article was written to call public attention to an early work by Rimsky-Korsakov. As time went on, Tchaikovsky was more frequently brought into personal rivalry with Korsakov than with any other member of the New Russian school. More than once they were engaged in actual public competition, and on several occasions chose the same subjects for their works. This in no way impaired their friendly relations, but the note of characteristic difference between them was accentuated with advancing years. Tchaikovsky himself, so frankly passionate in expression, was unable to understand the emotional reticence of Rimsky-Korsakov any more than that of Brahms. In both cases he attributes it to constitutional coldness and a lack of inspiration. The following paragraphs show how Tchaikovsky regarded the artistic development of Rimsky-Korsakov, who, as a lyric and symphonic composer, stood nearer to him, in some respects, than any other among his compatriots.

"The general impression of the symphony,"[1] he says, "may be resumed as follows : the predominance of technical skill over the quality of the ideas, and a lack of inspiration and fire.   In place of these, we have an elaborate design, with a superfluity of elegant details. This symphony seems to have been petted and coaxed into existence with the kind of maternal love which believes that all education consists in warming, feeding, and coddling the child.   Rimsky-Korsakov is apparently in a transition stage.   He is still seeking a point of support, still wavering between what is modern and a secret sympathy for old and archaic musical forms, which may be traced in him from the beginning.   This Philistine—a conservative at heart —has been enticed into the arena of the free-thinkers, and is timidly making his abjuration of faith.   As a result of this want of sincerity, Rimsky-Korsakov's recent works have become dry, cold, and formless ; a condition of things not always concealed by his elegant workmanship and minute stippling.   For this reason we cannot be surprised that the public do not receive his symphony with particular enthusiasm.

"Connoisseurs cannot fail to be delighted with the charming details and a play of sound-combinations so

[1] This criticism probably refers to the *Third Symphony* (op. 32).

flattering to the ear.   Through the two masks of the
Philistine and the innovator, which the composer
alternately dons without being able to decide frankly
to which side he belongs, we get constant glimpses of
a strong, highly gifted, elegantly plastic individuality.
When he has gone through this process of moral
fermentation, which apparently proceeds from his
inherent musical disposition, and has reached some
definite stage in his development, Rimsky-Korsakov
will certainly turn out one of the first symphonists of
the day.   But he will join the classical school to which
his musical nature inclines, rather than the formless
romantic school of Berlioz and Liszt.   Then he will
be a musical eclectic in the best sense of the word—
as Glinka was—uniting in himself strict classical forms
and methods with that dazzling beauty of modern
exposition, wherein lies the imprescriptible quality of
the new school."

Rimsky-Korsakov has not fulfilled Tchaikovsky's
prediction that he would eventually revert to classicism.
Starting with a knowledge of, and reverence for, formal
tradition, unique among the Russian composers, he has
nevertheless consistently followed the path which
attracted him most, the musical illustration of national
legend and national landscape.   Indeed the accusation
of wavering faith and want of sincerity comes strangely
from Tchaikovsky, who, from the beginning to the
end of his career, gave no signs of definite adherence
to the old forms or the new.   A glance at the list of
his works will show how, starting with a programme
symphony of a not very advanced type, he modified

his modern tendencies in the *Second Symphony* only to revert to them in *The Tempest*. Again, having written his *Third Symphony* under clearly conventional influences, he shows us in *Francesca di Rimini* that programme music still has its fascinations for his genius ; and so on, throughout the whole list of his opus numbers—*Manfred* following the *Fourth Symphony*, and *Hamlet* the *Fifth*. The same uncertainty characterises his use of national colour. Like so many of his fellow-countrymen, sometimes he uses foreign idioms with the fluency of a cosmopolitan, sometimes he speaks in a way that only Russians can understand. In this complex dual attitude lies much of Tchaikovsky's charm ; and much of his weakness—

> Oui, mon malheur irréparable,
> C'est de pendre aux deux éléments.

DIARY OF MY TOUR IN 1888

TRANSLATED FROM THE RUSSIAN

I

In 1886 it was proposed to produce my opera *Cherevichek* ("Two little Shoes") at the Great Theatre of Moscow. The scenery, elaborately designed by K. Valtz, was quite ready; all the superb mounting, upon which, during the previous year, I. A. Vsievolovsky had decided to expend a considerable sum, was complete, and the music was also finished. Meanwhile I—who was then residing in the country near Klin—lived in daily expectation of a summons to attend the first rehearsal in Moscow. But the season drew to its close, a few weeks only remained before Easter, and still the expected summons did not come. During that winter the business of the opera-house had been almost brought to a standstill in consequence of the prolonged illness of the conductor, I. K. Altani. At the beginning of December 1885 it was confidently believed that this respected artist, who was making a slow recovery to health, would soon return to his desk, where his place was filled by the chorus-master, Avranek, who had almost broken down under the strain of double work. But Altani's illness was variable, and the period of convalescence was obstinately prolonged. Just as I began to realise that *Cherevichek* was not likely to be offered to the judgment of the Moscow public during the season of 1885-86, and had concluded that the performance must be postponed for some future season, an unexpected offer was made to the directors by a young musician in Moscow, who professed his readiness to take Altani's place and produce my complicated score at some date in the immediate future. The offer was at once communicated to me, and M. P. M. Pchelnikov, then the head of the theatrical administration, begged me to say if I had sufficient confidence in this substitute to entrust him with the rehearsing and conducting of *Cherevichek*. As I set a high value on Altani's friendliness to me as a composer, and also esteemed his remarkable talent and experience, I promptly declined the proposal of this young musician to take the place of my respected friend at the conductor's desk. At the same time, as I did not wish to put any obstacle in the way of the directors, if it seemed to their advantage to give an immediate performance of my opera, I adopted the heroic measure of offering my own services as conductor. They thanked me cordially, and accepted my proposal. But finally a combination of different circumstances made the performance impossible during the season of 1885-86.

The following season, when the staging of *Chere-*

vichek came once more under consideration, Altani
had completely regained his health, and there appeared
no need whatever for me to attempt to act as
conductor. Nevertheless the chiefs of the theatrical
administration, and Altani himself, as well as my
numerous friends in Moscow, still wished me to
conduct the rehearsal and the first public performance
of my opera in person. It had long been the pre-
valent opinion that I had no gift whatever for
conducting ; and I myself clung obstinately to the
belief that I was completely incapable—so much so,
that my timid efforts, on two separate occasions, to
conquer my morbid nervousness and appear before
the public had ended most disastrously in my entire
discomfiture. If, however, my well-wishers, including Altani, desired, in spite of this, to make me
overcome my diffidence, and were anxious that I
should make one more effort, in my declining years,
to become a conductor, they were doubtless guided
by sincere affection and by a strong conviction that
my lack of talent as a conductor was a great hindrance
to the spread of my works, and believed that if I
once conquered myself and succeeded in conducting—
if only tolerably—some of my compositions, the result
would be a great impulse to the popularising of my
music and a rapid increase of my fame as a composer.

Fortified by the warm sympathy of my friends,
and the invaluable advice and guidance of Altani,
as well as by my entire confidence in the indulgence
of the Moscow public, who had encouraged my
first efforts as a composer, and, since that time, had

invariably shown me the most cordial sympathy—on 19th January 1887, at 8 P.M., I took the conductor's place in the orchestra of the Great Opera House, and successfully conducted the first performance of *Cherevichek*. I was then forty-seven years of age. At this time of life a real, inborn conductor has plenty of capacity, in proportion to his natural gifts and length of experience ; when it is borne in mind that such was not the case with me, my *début* may be considered exceedingly successful. I still think that I have no positive gift for conducting. I am aware that I do not possess that combination of moral and physical qualities which make an ordinary musician a conductor of the first rank ; but this attempt—and all subsequent ones—proved that I could more or less successfully direct the performance of my works, and this was all that was necessary for my future success. I have considered it important to relate in detail the story of my first attempt at conducting, because among the many good results which it led to was the three months' concert tour which I made through Western Europe. Of the success which attended this tour I cannot fail to be proud, and I afterwards resolved to relate the details to the Russian public ; for, with the exception of Glinka, who gave but one concert in Paris, and Rubinstein, who, thanks to his gifts as a virtuoso, won laurels on all the platforms of the world, I was the first Russian to introduce my works personally abroad. I venture to think that there are a considerable number of Russians to whom this account will be of interest.

II

Six weeks after the events related above, when experience had proved me to possess sufficient capability to conduct opera, I made a similar attempt on the concert platform. On 4th March 1887 I conducted a concert given in the Salle de la Noblesse, St. Petersburg, by the Philharmonic Society, the programme of which consisted entirely of my compositions. The experiment was crowned with success. To my great astonishment, I heard from those in whose judgment I have the fullest confidence such flattering opinions of my conducting that my heart beat for joy, and I could not help feeling proud of having won a victory over myself, and over that desperate, cruel, tyrannical, moral ailment against which I had contended all my life—namely, nervousness. Only one well-known musical critic showed no moderation in his judgment of me. He had hailed my *début* as a composer in the following words: "M. Tchaikovsky is very poor; he has not a spark of talent." This is very severe; but he equally distorted the truth when he said I was an "admirable" conductor. However, I did not believe him on this occasion any more than I believed his earlier statement as to my absolute want of talent. Men who first take up the conductor's baton at forty-seven cannot possibly be "admirable" conductors; indeed it is useless to hope that they will become such, even if they have the necessary natural endowment; and I am perfectly aware that innate nervousness, weakness of character, and want of self-confidence will always prevent me from competing with such conductors as Wagner, Bülow, and Napravnik. Only one thing, I repeat, was of importance to me: to be able to conduct my own works no worse than any other mediocre conductor would have done. I foresaw that, thanks to this victory over my incapacity, it would now be possible for me to make my music known at home and abroad, and very soon my premonition became actual fact.

In June I received an invitation from the Hamburg Philharmonic Society to conduct some of my works in the following January. Afterwards I received similar invitations from Vienna, Dresden, Copenhagen, Prague, Leipzig, Berlin, and London. As regards Paris, Felix Mackar—a great enthusiast for my music—had already promised that I should appear there as conductor at a concert which he wished to organise during the winter season.

A very natural ambition to extend as far as possible the circle of my fame as a composer did not prevent me from cherishing a hope that I might also succeed in serving the cause of Russian art, and popularise the works of other Russian composers on my travels. Imagining that I possessed sufficient funds to risk giving a Russian concert in Paris on my own account, at which should figure the names of Glinka, Dargomijsky, Serov, Rubinstein, Balakirev, Rimsky-Korsakov, Glazounov, Liadov, and Arensky, I firmly resolved to follow up the concert arranged by Felix Mackar, at which only my music was to be performed, by another consisting of the works of these stars. It was extremely flattering and agreeable to think that I might be the one to interpret these gems of Russian music to a French public imbued and inspired with sympathy for everything Russian. The evening before my departure, I spent some hours in the society of three of my most valued musical friends, Rimsky-Korsakov, Liadov, and Glazounov, with whom I worked out in every detail the programme of the enterprise I meditated carrying out. Thus, in quitting Petersburg I had three ends in view—to conduct my own works in Leipzig and other foreign towns, and to conduct two concerts in Paris, one of which was to be devoted to my own works, and the other to be organised at my own risk.

For two months preceding my departure I had also been in correspondence with a certain Herr N., a concert-agent abroad, who showed himself most zealous in the propagation of my works out of Russia, going so far as to consider it practicable for me to visit a whole series of second-rate towns in Germany and Austria, because he had formed a very exaggerated estimate of the interest which my music awakened in these neighbouring empires. But, realising with consternation that Herr N. was going too far in his zeal, I declined to accept—whether he liked it or not—his proposal for a personal interview which was to take place in Germany. When later on it actually did take place, it seemed to me that I had to do with a very peculiar and eccentric man, and from that moment to this I have never really understood him. Whether from inexperience or misapprehension, or from a natural want of practical ability and tact, or simply from some abnormal, morbid condition of mind, in any case Herr N. was very unreliable, and being apparently my devoted friend, his actions were sometimes those of an enemy. He did me many important services, for which I shall never cease to be grateful, but he was also the cause of several serious unpleasantnesses and annoyances that befell me during my tour. Thus, even now, I cannot form any just opinion upon this singular man, who remains altogether an enigma to me. I was equally puzzled as to his nationality— he called himself Russian, but spoke the language atrociously—his position in the world, and more especially as to the motive which guided his conduct towards me, now persecuting me with hostile proceedings, now rendering me the most valuable service. In any case, I must acknowledge that it was entirely due to his initiative that I owed my invitations to Leipzig, Prague, and Copenhagen. This last city I did not succeed in visiting, because I had not time ; while the concert at Dresden never even came off, in consequence of Herr N.'s strange and unpractical management. Nor was it my luck to make the Viennese acquainted with my music, because the day fixed for the concert in Vienna was identical with the date on which I had to be in Paris. Finally, the incomprehensible and eccentric fancy of Herr N.'s to compel me to wander through a series of little German towns, conducting a miniature orchestra which was quite incapable of rendering my difficult and complicated scores, was, needless to say, never realised. The Russian concert I meditated giving in Paris proved a childishly impossible dream, about which I will speak more fully elsewhere. Thus it happened that I only visited Leipzig, Hamburg, Berlin, Prague, Paris, and London. I now return to my story.

III

I LEFT St. Petersburg on 15th (27th) December, and arrived in Berlin on the 17th (29th). Here I wished to interview the director (Vorsteher) of the Berlin Philharmonic Society, Herr Schneider, who had been corresponding with me about the concert in February, which was to consist entirely of my works, and at which I was to act as conductor. A personal interview was necessary in order to discuss the details of the programme, and the matter presented some difficulties, for Schneider, who desired for my own interests to please the Berlin public, did not altogether agree with my selection of works. He wished to include some that I did not care for, and at the same time to omit those of which I was most proud, and by which the splendid Berlin orchestra might have shown me at my best. However, this time I did not succeed in seeing Herr Schneider, for the following reason. In the newspaper which the waiter brought with my tea I read, with horror, the following lines about my arrival: "To-day, 29th January, the Russian composer Tchaikovsky arrives in Berlin. His numerous friends (?) and admirers (?) will assemble to celebrate his arrival by a *Fruhschapp* (breakfast) at —— Restaurant, in such-and-such a street, at —— o'clock." I must explain that Herr N. had already spoken of this *Fruhschapp* in a letter to me at Petersburg, and had even sent me a copy of the circular which he had distributed through Berlin, in which all music-lovers, artists, and fellow-countrymen of mine living in the town were invited to assemble at a certain hour in one of the best-known restaurants, because Herr N. informed them that I was exceedingly modest, and wished the welcome to be of quite a friendly and intimate character. On receiving this letter I telegraphed immediately to Herr N. that I distinctly declined to take part in this festivity, and that I would not on any account appear at this friendly *Fruhschapp*. Therefore I was beyond measure incensed when I now saw in the paper that he had not dropped the matter, but even published this on the day of my arrival. Luckily Herr N. did not know where I was staying, and I decided not to let him know of my arrival until the next day. I think it will be clear to most of my readers why this proceeding on the part of Herr N.—who sincerely wished to render me a service, but had a most singular notion of how to do it—covered me with confusion, horror, and fright. But to such of my readers as know little or nothing of the attitude of the foreign public towards Russian composers, I will merely say that not only had I very few admirers in Berlin, but that previously to this my music was almost unknown there. A few of my orchestral works had been occasionally heard, it is true. Bilze, at his National Concerts, had often played the *Andante* from my Quartet ; but the whole acquaintance of the Berliners with my music was limited to these few bars ; and as to my "numerous friends and admirers," I was a complete stranger in Berlin. With the exceptions of the head of the firm of Bote and Bock, Herr Hugo Bock, I had not a single acquaintance. Moreover there could be no question of admirers, for the few things of mine which had hitherto been performed in Berlin had had no particular success, and the Press had not been unanimous in its praise. This puffery of Herr N.'s, this idea of honouring me in Berlin by means of a *Fruhschapp*, is the best example of his queer, unmethodical, flighty way of acting on my behalf. Yet he was, to all appearances, really well-intentioned, and with incredible zeal, energy, and eccentricity, devoted all his time and thought to making my name familiar to the German public. The result of all this was that I felt almost ashamed of myself. It seemed to me that all the musical world of Berlin would be laughing at me, and thinking perhaps that *I* wanted, through the medium of Herr N., to get up this festive reception which I did not merit. I felt no further desire to see any one in the German capital, and the next day, having seen and tried to explain to Herr N., and after visiting K. V. Davidov—who was then passing through Berlin, and whom it was a great pleasure to meet again—I started for Leipzig, from whence I began my tour through Western Europe.

IV

IN Leipzig I met three compatriots and one German critic. My fellow‑countrymen were: Brodsky, Siloti, and Arthur Friedheim. The two first are very well known to the Russian public, especially in Moscow. I had long been on intimate terms with Brodsky, who was for some time a professor at the Moscow Conservatoire when I took the theory class there. In 1877 Brodsky left Moscow, spent one season at Kiev as director of the Musical Society, and, after travelling about for a considerable time, was finally appointed to the honourable post of Professor of the Violin at the Leipzig Conservatoire, where he won universal affection and esteem both as a man and as an artist. In speaking of this admirable master, I must take this opportunity of expressing in public the sincere gratitude which I shall feel for him till my dying day. The reason is as follows. In 1877 I wrote a violin concerto which I dedicated to Auer. I do not know whether my dedication was flattering to Herr Auer, but, in spite of his genuine friendship, he never tried to conquer the difficulties of this concerto. He pronounced it impossible to play, and this verdict, coming from such an authority as the Petersburg virtuoso, had the effect of casting this unfortunate child of my imagination for many years to come into the limbo of hopelessly forgotten things. Five years later, however, I was staying in Rome, and going into a café, chanced to pick up a number of the *Neue Freie Presse* containing a criticism, by the celebrated Hanslick, of a concert given by the Vienna Philharmonic Society, the programme of which included my unlucky concerto, which Auer's verdict had doomed to extinction. Hanslick found fault with the player (who was none other than Brodsky himself) for his unfortunate selection, and cut up my poor concerto unmercifully, not sparing the pearls of his caustic humour, nor the poisoned arrows of his sarcasm. "We know," he writes, " that certain works have recently appeared in contemporary literature, the authors of which delight in reproducing certain revolting physiological phenomena, as, for example, disgusting smells. Such literature may be well termed — stinking. Tchaikovsky's concerto appears to us to belong to the category of 'stinking music.'" On reading this notice by the celebrated and influential critic, I called up a lively picture of all the energy and pains that Brodsky must have expended in carrying out this performance of my "stinking" concerto, and thought how annoying and unpleasant he would find this kind criticism upon a friend and compatriot. I hastened, therefore, to express my warmest gratitude to Brodsky, and learnt from the letter he wrote in reply what difficulties and trials he had gone through in order to accomplish his aim—the resuscitation of my concerto from the depths of oblivion.　After-wards Brodsky played the "stinking concerto" everywhere, and everywhere the critics abused him in the same style as Hanslick.　But the deed was done ; my concerto was saved, and is now frequently played in Western Europe, especially since there came to Brodsky's assistance another fine violinist, young Halir, of whom I shall often have occasion to speak. It will now be evident how pleased I was to meet Brodsky in Leipzig, where I was a stranger without friends, and to look forward, amid the fears and agitations which beset me, to the moral support of his long-standing and intimate friendship.

Not less glad was I to see once more that young, but already celebrated, pianist Siloti.　I had known him when a mere boy, a pupil of the Moscow Con-servatoire, where he went through some finishing courses in composition under my guidance.　Since then Siloti, who had studied the piano under Nicholas Rubinstein, and after his death under Liszt, had won a great name in Russia and Germany, especially in Leipzig, where he had been living for several years, visiting other German and Russian cities from time to time.　This young artist, like Brodsky, rendered me many a friendly service, and did a great deal towards making my works known in Germany. Thanks to him, I found in Leipzig a circle of musicians who did me the honour of showing great

interest in my music. This was of great importance
to me, for I entered Leipzig—a town renowned for
its violent conservatism in general and its rabid anti-
Russian feeling in particular—as into a hostile camp,
with the sense of attracting all its insolence and
derision to myself. Of course there was some
exaggeration in this feeling, for, as the reader will
presently see, the Germans as a rule do not hate us
so outrageously as many think. But it is a fact that
I suffered a great deal from the consciousness of this
fancied enmity in Leipzig, and that it was very
consoling to find some amateurs among its inhabit-
ants who knew my music and felt a genuine sympathy for it—and for its composer.

The third fellow-countryman whom I met in
Leipzig was Arthur Friedheim, a talented pianist and
pupil of Liszt's, a native of Petersburg, who had been
living for some time in Leipzig. As regards the
German who came to the station in order to receive
me, he was Martin Krause, the influential critic of
the Leipzig *Tageblatt*, an intimate friend of Siloti's,
who took a very gratifying interest in my music.

I found, on my arrival at Leipzig, the same really
severe winter weather as in Russia. Snow lay thick
in the streets, and I went almost straight from the
station—in a little sledge very ingeniously contrived
—to a Christmas Tree at Brodsky's. I found him
established in thoroughly Russian surroundings, and
these were further graced by the presence of two very
sympathetic Russian ladies, the wife and sister-in-law
of my host. During recent years I had hardly ever

left home, and being quite unaccustomed to stay away from my country for long together, I felt restless and homesick ; therefore no words will describe the comfort I derived, both that evening and subsequently, during my three different visits to Leipzig, whenever I had occasion to spend a few hours in Mr. Brodsky's family.   I was also very pleased to visit Siloti, who had not long since married a young lady whom I had known almost as a child in Moscow, and with whom I had long been on terms of intimate friendship.

V

THE next day I made two very interesting acquaintances. Going to Brodsky's for the one o'clock
dinner, I heard sounds of the piano, violin, and
'cello. They were rehearsing for the next day's
performance of Brahms's new Pianoforte Trio (op.
100), and the composer himself was at the piano.
Thus it chanced that I saw the famous German
musician for the first time. Brahms is rather a short
man, suggests a sort of amplitude, and possesses
a very sympathetic appearance. His fine head,
almost that of an old man, recalls the type of a
handsome, benign, elderly Russian priest. His
features are certainly not characteristic of Russian
good looks, and I cannot conceive why some learned
ethnographer (Brahms himself told me this after I
had spoken of the impression his appearance made
upon me) chose to reproduce his head on the first
page of one of his books as being highly characteristic of German features. A certain softness of
outline, pleasing curves, rather long and slightly
grizzled hair, kind grey eyes, and a thick beard

freely sprinkled with white—all this recalled at once the type of pure-bred Great Russian, so frequently met with among our clergy.

Brahms's manner is very simple, free from vanity, his humour jovial, and the few hours spent in his society left me with a very agreeable recollection. Unfortunately I was forced to confess that, in spite of a somewhat prolonged stay among them in Leipzig, I had not got on very well with the most prominent representatives of modern German music. The reason was as follows. Like all my Russian musical friends, without exception, I only respected in Brahms an honourable, energetic musician of strong convictions ; but, in spite of all efforts to the contrary, I never could, and never can, admire his music. Brahmsism is very widespread throughout Germany ; there are a number of authoritative people and an entire musical institution specially consecrated to the Brahms cult, and he is considered a great man, almost the equal of Beethoven. But there are anti-Brahmsites in Germany and everywhere beyond the German frontier, with the exception, perhaps, of London, where, thanks to the energetic propaganda of Joachim, who is very popular in England, the greatness of Brahms is recognised to a certain extent. Everywhere else, as I say, there reigns complete ignorance and ignoring of Brahms. But nowhere, perhaps, has he made less way than in Russia. There is something dry, cold, vague, and nebulous in the music of this master which is repellent to Russian hearts. From our Russian point of view Brahms does not possess melodic invention. His musical ideas never speak to the point; hardly have we heard an allusion to some tangible melodic phrase than it disappears in a whirlpool of almost unmeaning harmonic progressions and modulations, as though the composer's special aim was to be incomprehensible and obscure. Thus he excites and irritates our musical perceptions, as it were, yet is unwilling to satisfy their demands; he seems ashamed, to put it plainly, to speak clearly and reach the heart. Hearing his music, we ask ourselves : Is Brahms deep, or does he only desire to have the semblance of depth in order to mask the poverty of his imagination? This question is never satisfactorily answered.

It is impossible in listening to Brahms's music to say that it is weak or unremarkable. His style is always elevated. Unlike all our contemporary musicians, he never has recourse to purely external effects ; he never attempts to astonish us, to strike us by some new and brilliant orchestral combination ; nor do we meet in his music with anything trivial or directly imitative. It is all very serious, very distinguished, apparently even original, but in spite of all this the chief thing is lacking—beauty ! This is my view of Brahms, and as far as I know it is shared by all Russian composers and all the musical public of Russia. A few years ago, when I frankly expressed my opinion of Brahms to Hans von Bülow, he replied : " Wait awhile, the time will come when you will enter into the depth and beauty of Brahms.

Like you, it was long before I understood him, but gradually I was blessed by the revelation of his genius. It will be the same with you." And still I wait ; but the revelation tarries. I deeply revere the artistic personality of Brahms. I bow to the actual purity of his musical tendencies, and admire his firm and proud renunciation of all the tricks which solemnise the Wagnerian cult, and in a much less degree the worship of Liszt, but I do not care for his music.

My readers will see that this fact prevented my seeking for an intimate acquaintance with the very attractive personality of Brahms. I met him in the society of devoted partisans (of whom Brodsky is one), and it appeared to me unseemly—seeing that I was a stranger and did not share in the worship of their idol—to bring any discordant element into the complete harmony of these intensely devout believers in this musical dogma. Brahms himself, as though he distinctly understood, or was actually aware of, the fact that I did not belong to his camp, made no effort to become intimate. He was quite simple and polite to me as to every one else, but nothing more. Meanwhile, all that I have heard of Brahms as a man has made me doubly regret that the " revelation " predicted by von Bülow has not been vouchsafed to me. He is an unusually pleasing and attractive man, and all who have come in contact with him are inspired by a warm affection and devotion. The celebrated Czechist composer Dvorak used to speak with tears in his eyes of the warm interest Brahms showed him at a time when his compositions found neither publishers nor performers, and what powerful support he gave him, and what energy he showed in sounding the depths of unknown genius of his Slavonic brother in art! Brodsky also related instances which revealed the sympathetic side of Brahms's character, especially his rare and pleasing modesty. It is well known that Wagner treated his contemporaries with the greatest animosity, and always showed himself particularly caustic to Brahms's works. Once, when some one reported to the latter some fresh sarcasm which Wagner had levelled at him, he exclaimed: "Good heavens! Wagner, honoured and triumphant, takes up most of the high-road. How can I, going my own modest way, be any hindrance or annoyance to him? Why cannot he leave me in peace, since we are never likely to clash?"

VI

At this same dinner at Brodsky's I made another acquaintance, not less interesting, but deeper and less fleeting than the first, and destined soon to be transformed into a genuine friendship, based upon the undoubted affinity of two musical natures, though neither of us was well acquainted with the other's works. During the rehearsal of Brahms's new trio, as I was taking the liberty of making some remarks as to the skill and execution of the relative *tempo* 2-3—remarks which were very good-naturedly received by the composer—there entered the room a very short, middle-aged man, exceedingly fragile in appearance, with shoulders of unequal height, fair hair brushed back from his forehead, and a very slight, almost boyish, beard and moustache. There was nothing very striking about the features of this man, whose exterior at once attracted my sympathy, for it would be impossible to call them handsome or regular ; but he had an uncommon charm, and blue eyes, not very large, but irresistibly fascinating, recalling the glance of a charming and candid child.

I rejoiced in the depths of my heart when we were mutually introduced to each other, and it turned out that this personality which was so inexplicably sympathetic to me belonged to a musician whose warmly emotional music had long ago won my heart. He proved to be the Norwegian composer Edward Grieg, who twenty years earlier had gained great popularity in Russia and the Scandinavian Peninsula, and together with Svendsen had acquired the highest respect and a great name. I think I am right in saying that just as Brahms was undeservedly disliked by the Russian musicians and general public, so Grieg had known how to win over Russian hearts once and for all. In his music there prevails that fascinating melancholy which seems to reflect in itself all the beauty of Norwegian scenery, now grandiose and sublime in its vast expanse, now grey and dull, but always full of charm to the hearts of Northmen, and having something akin to ourselves, quickly finds its way to our hearts, and evokes a warm and sympathetic response.

Grieg is probably not by any means so great a master as Brahms ; his range is not so extensive, his aims and tendencies are not so wide, and apparently in Grieg the inclination towards obscurity is entirely absent ; nevertheless he stands nearer to us, he seems more approachable and intelligible because of his deep humanity. Hearing the music of Grieg, we instinctively recognise that it was written by a man impelled by an irresistible impulse to give vent by means of sounds to a flood of poetical emotion, which obeys no theory or principle, is stamped with no impress but that of a vigorous and sincere artistic feeling.   Perfection of form, strict and irreproachable logic in the development of his themes, are not perseveringly sought after by the celebrated Norwegian.   But what charm, what inimitable and rich musical imagery!   What warmth and passion in his melodic phrases, what teeming vitality in his harmony, what originality and beauty in the turn of his piquant and ingenious modulations and rhythms, and in all the rest what interest, novelty, and independence!   If we add to all this that rarest of qualities, a perfect simplicity, far removed from all affectation and pretence to obscurity and far-fetched novelty (and many contemporary composers, including some Russians, are striving with a morbid tendency to break into new ways without possessing the least vocation or natural gift), it is not surprising that every one should delight in Grieg, that he should be popular everywhere — in Paris, London, and Moscow—that his name should appear in all concert programmes, and that visitors to Bergen should deem it a pleasant duty to make a pilgrimage to the charming though remote haven among the rocks of the shore, where Grieg retires to work and where he spends most of his life.

I trust it will not appear like self-glorification that my dithyramb in praise of Grieg precedes the statement that our natures are closely allied.   Speaking of Grieg's high qualities, I do not at all wish to impress my readers with the notion that I am endowed with an equal share of them. I leave it to others to decide how far I am lacking in all that Grieg possesses in such abundance, but I cannot help stating the fact that he exercises and has exercised some measure of that attractive force which always drew me towards the gifted Norwegian. Later on I shall have occasion to prove this ; meanwhile I will only say that I value Grieg's sympathy very highly, and thank my lucky star for this meeting and opportunity of personal acquaintance with him.

Together with Grieg, there entered the room where we were assembled a lady who was growing slightly grey and resembled him very closely in appearance, being just as small, fragile, and sympathetic. She was his wife, and also his cousin, which accounts for their resemblance. Subsequently I was able to appreciate the many and precious qualities possessed by Madame Grieg. In the first place she proved to be an excellent, though not very finished, singer ; secondly, I have never met a better-informed or more highly-cultivated woman, and she is, among other things, an excellent judge of our literature, in which Grieg himself was also deeply interested ; thirdly, I was soon convinced that Madame Grieg was as amiable, as gentle, as childishly simple and without guile as her celebrated husband.

There was another lady at this party about whom I should like to say a few words. After the Christmas Tree, while we were all sitting round the tea-table at Brodsky's, a beautiful dog of the setter breed came bounding into the room and began to frisk round the host and his little nephew, who welcomed his arrival. "This means that Miss Smyth will appear directly," everybody exclaimed at once, and in a few minutes a tall Englishwoman, not handsome, but having what people call an "expressive" or "intelligent" face, walked into the room, and I was introduced to her at once as a fellow-composer. Miss Smyth is one of the comparatively few women composers who may be seriously reckoned among the workers in this sphere of music. She had come to Leipzig a few years before and studied theory and composition very thoroughly; she had composed several interesting works (the best of which, a violin sonata, I heard excellently played by the composer herself and Mr. Brodsky), and gave promise in the future of a serious and talented career. Since no Englishwoman is without her originalities and eccentricities, Miss Smyth had hers, which were: the beautiful dog, which was quite inseparable from this lonely woman, and invariably announced her arrival, not only on this occasion, but at other times when I met her again; a passion for hunting, on account of which Miss Smyth occasionally returned to England for a time; and, finally, an incomprehensible and almost passionate worship for the intangible musical genius of Brahms. From her point of view Brahms stood on the supreme pinnacle of all music, and all that had gone before him served merely as a preparation for the incarnation of absolute musical beauty in the creations of the Viennese master. And in this case, as invariably, when I came in contact with rabid Brahmsites, I tormented myself with the question : Are they all wrong and imagine what does not exist, or have I so offended God and Nature that the "revelation" predicted by Bülow will never condescend to bless me ?

The first day of 1888 (New Style) fell at this period, so full of varied impressions, and that day I was present at an extra concert at the Gewandhaus, at which a new work by Brahms—his *Double Concerto for Violin and 'Cello*—was played for the first time.   Joachim played the violin, the 'cello was taken by the celebrated Berlin virtuoso Haussmann, and Brahms himself conducted the orchestra. The concerto, notwithstanding its excellent rendering, produced no impression upon me whatever.   I was struck by the absolute perfection with which the famous choir of the Thomaskirche—consisting of men's and boys' voices—sang a number of choruses *à capella*, among them a motet by J. S. Bach.   I never heard anything like it at home, and I confess that I was unpleasantly surprised, for I had hitherto believed that some of our first-rate choirs were the very best in the world.   The performance of Beethoven's *Fifth Symphony* by the splendid Gewandhaus orchestra would have quite sent me into ecstasies if it had not been that the respected conductor, Herr Reinecke, took the *tempi* too slow, as I thought.   Perhaps he was justified by the true traditions ; if so, it is better not to keep them too strictly, for I am firmly persuaded that this inspired symphony is better and more charming when taken quicker, as with us. The hall of the new Gewandhaus is very fine, and holds a large audience ; it is lit by electric light, is comfortable, beautiful, elegant, and, most important of all, possesses exemplary acoustic arrangements. In the large box belonging to the directors, in which I sat, were many distinguished members of the Leipzig musical world, with all of whom I was acquainted, and among them Reinecke, who was very attentive to me. The head of the Concert Society of the Gewandhaus, Herr Linburger, informed me that my first rehearsal would take place the following morning at ten o'clock.

VII

THE famous Gewandhaus concerts, given in connection with the little town of Leipzig, which is one of the first musical centres of Germany, are celebrated for the excellence of the symphony orchestra, and distinguished by their conservative and classical programmes, in which—apart from the three great classical composers, Haydn, Mozart, Beethoven, and their contemporaries—only Mendelssohn and Schumann are recognised. The works of Wagner, Berlioz, and Liszt are rarely performed there. It is only very recently that the directors of this musical institution have begun to make some timid advances in the spirit of the times, and one of these moves was my unexpected invitation to Leipzig in order to conduct one of my own works. Both in Germany and at home this invitation excited considerable surprise ; but especially in the former country, where many people, without any real foundation, regard me as a representative of the ultra-revolutionary party in music, just as in Russia I am often placed, equally without grounds, in the ranks of the retrogrades. Probably the event would never have come off but for the kind intercession of Mr. Brodsky, who has great influence in Leipzig ; but the initiative in this instance is due to Herr N., of whom I have already spoken. In any case I recognise the fact, in all sincerity, that the choice of a work of mine in the Gewandhaus programmes was very flattering to my vanity as a composer, and that I was exceedingly glad to be starting my tour from Leipzig, because this incident was sure to lend greater weight to my name throughout Germany. But the prouder I felt of this attention from the Direction of the Gewandhaus, the more anxious I was to prove a worthy representative of Russian music abroad, and the more indescribably was I agitated by my inherent shyness and the fear " lest I should do something to blush for." After a night of misery, disturbed by every possible apprehension, and particularly by the dread lest my nervousness should prevent my doing myself justice as a passable conductor, I started for the rehearsal, accompanied by Siloti. As we approached the Gewandhaus, we met, at the entrance, the respected Capellmeister, Reinecke, who was hurrying in to the rehearsal in order to introduce me to the orchestra. In Germany and throughout Europe, Reinecke enjoys the reputation of being an excellent musician and a talented composer of the school of Mendelssohn. He is a skilful conductor of the Gewandhaus concerts ; that is to say, he conducts them in a worthy manner, but not with that especial brilliance which has made them so famous throughout the world.

I say "not with especial brilliance," because many
Germans deny that Reinecke possesses talent as a
conductor, and would like to see his place filled by a
musician of a more impassioned temperament, of
stronger and more decided character. At any rate
he is one of the most prominent and influential
members of the German musical world, and if there
are not a few Wagnerians, Lisztites, Brahmsites, and
other progressists of all shades who do not love
Reinecke, none refuse to respect him as a capable
and conscientious musician. Such a respect I, too,
had long since felt for Reinecke, and now the unusual attention and kindness which he hastened to
show, both at the extra concert at the Gewandhaus
and during my entire visit to Leipzig, were of the
greatest value to me.

When the Capelldiener announced that all the
musicians were assembled, we went from the artists'
room to the platform ; Reinecke took me to the
conductor's desk, tapped with the baton, spoke a few
words of introduction, to which the musicians replied
by clapping and rapping on their desks with their
bows, and handed me the baton. I then stepped
into the conductor's place, spoke a few complimentary words, probably in very bad German, and the
rehearsal began, Reinecke now quitting the room.
We played my *First Suite*, in five movements, of
which the first (Introduction and Fugue) is considered
one of my most successful efforts. The first quarter of
an hour of this rehearsal, before I had had time to take
in all the strange faces in the orchestra, was very

trying and agitating, at least for such a nervous and inexperienced conductor as myself. Only after the first break, when I had to set right some misunderstandings, I was able to look more closely at the members of the orchestra, — then the nervousness passed off, and there remained only my anxiety to make the business go as well as possible. After the first movement of the *Suite*, I could see by their looks and smiles that many of the players were already friendly towards me. At this the last traces of shyness vanished, the whole rehearsal went off very pleasantly, and I came away with the conviction that I had to deal with an orchestra of extraordinary capability. Both Reinecke and Brahms were present at the rehearsal. On meeting Brahms, he made no encouraging remarks ; I was told he was very pleased with the first movement, but did not praise the rest, especially the " Marche Miniature."

The next rehearsal was a general one. It is the custom in Leipzig to admit the public to this final rehearsal, and this audience consists chiefly of young students, who are very warm and generous in the expression of their feelings, while the audience at the concerts themselves is exceedingly cold, critical, and chary of its praise. At the rehearsal my *Suite* and its composer were honoured by a storm of applause and by repeated recalls. But this was perhaps entirely owing to the presence of a great number of Russian students in philology, who were not sparing in the loud expression of their feelings for a fellow-countryman. In any case I was very pleased with my success, and on returning home I was to experience a still greater pleasure. This took the form of a card which Grieg had left for me on his way back from the rehearsal, with a few written words in which the impression the *Suite* had made upon him was expressed with such warmth and enthusiasm that I scruple to repeat them to my readers. A sincere compliment from such a gifted *confrère* as Grieg is the highest and most precious joy that can fall to an artist's lot.

The next day the concert itself took place. Mr. Brodsky had previously prepared me for a chilly reception by the audience, therefore I was neither surprised nor annoyed when on mounting to the conductor's desk there was not a single clap, and the sole response to my bow was a sepulchral silence. But after the first movement followed lively applause, more or less repeated after each succeeding movement of the *Suite*, and at the end I was twice recalled, which, at the Gewandhaus, may be interpreted as the proof of a great success. After the concert I went to supper with Reinecke. He and his family all did their best to be kind and polite ; and Herr Reinecke, who among other things is an excellent French scholar, proved exceedingly agreeable and charming in conversation. In his youth he had been intimate with Schumann, and related many incidents in the life of the great German master. Schumann was really melancholy, and it might have been predicted from the first that this inherent depression would lead to hypochondria and insanity, as it eventually did. He was surprisingly silent ; it seemed as though every word cost him an extraordinary effort. What was peculiarly striking in his musical organisation was his complete lack of power as a conductor, and Reinecke told me of an instance which made it evident that he could not even distinguish accurately the various *timbres* of orchestral instruments, and that he was entirely wanting in a natural feeling for rhythm, so indispensable for a conductor. How difficult to realise such an anomaly in a musician who, judging from his works, was so especially inventive as regards rhythm !

At Reinecke's I made the acquaintance of the French composer Gouvies, who always spent the winter in Leipzig. Monsieur Gouvies was completely Teutonised, spoke German perfectly, was rather hostile towards his own country (that is as regards music), and on the whole gave me the unpleasant impression of a man who thinks himself disillusioned and injured, and not being appreciated by his own countrymen, is consequently disposed to exaggerate the virtues and value of foreigners. It is quite probable that Monsieur Gouvies had some good cause for railing against musical France ; but it was painful to me to hear him extol everything German at the expense of France. I had never met such a type of Frenchman before.

VIII

ANOTHER day (Christmas Day itself, according to
Russian style) I was present at a concert given by
the Liszt-Verein in the room of the old Gewandhaus.
Just in proportion as the new concert-room is beautiful, sumptuous, roomy, and elegant, the old one is
small, uncomfortable, and even rather dirty. But
this room, and especially the little artists' room
attached to it, has sacred memories in German art,
and a thrill of awe passed through me when, seated
there, I thought how its walls had often looked upon
Mendelssohn, Schumann, and many other great
musicians who had appeared, through many decades,
upon the platform of the Gewandhaus.

The concert took place in the morning, and consisted exclusively of my works. The society which
bears the name of Liszt, contrary to the Gewandhaus,
devotes all its energies to the production of modern
music. It has only been in existence two years, but
already it has its own public, a fairly large one, which
on this occasion filled the hall to the last seat. Among
the directors of this society are many admirers of

Liszt, mostly young people of energy and talent, and it seems as though, in time, it might become a serious rival to the Gewandhaus. Among those who are particularly delighted with the success of the society, I must mention the talented musical critics Martin Krause and Fritsch, the gifted conductor of the Leipzig Opera (a native of Vienna), and our fellow-countryman Siloti.

The leader of the Grand Ducal orchestra of Weimar came from that town on purpose to hear this concert. The young violinist Halir, of whom I had heard so much from his admirer Siloti, and whose acquaintance I was all the more pleased to make because in recent years he had made a special study of my violin concerto—the one I have already alluded to in connection with Brodsky—took part in the concert. Halir had played my concerto everywhere, enduring the sneers and censure of the most influential critics upon his queer taste, and striving, in spite of all this, to make my much-abused creation one of the show-pieces at symphony concerts in Germany. On this occasion Herr Halir, together with Siloti and that excellent 'cellist Schroeder (who has since had a great success in Moscow), played my Trio dedicated to the memory of Nicholas Rubinstein. The rendering was quite exemplary. Herr Petri's quartet (he is the leader of the Gewandhaus orchestra) played my first quartet very finely, and, besides these, one or two smaller compositions of mine were performed. The audience of the Liszt-Verein are enthusiastic and very generous in their applause. I could not complain of any lack of warmth. The society presented me with a wreath. During the whole performance I sat on the platform in full view of the audience, having Grieg and his wife as neighbours. Afterwards a friendly critic— Fritsch—told me that he saw a lady point out the Griegs and myself to her daughter, saying, "Look, dear, there sits Tchaikovsky, and by his side his children." This was said quite seriously, and is not so very surprising, because I am quite grey and elderly, while Grieg, who is forty-five, and his wife, look extraordinarily young and small at a distance.

After the concert I spent some very pleasant hours with Siloti and some friends of his, directors of the Liszt-Verein. We talked a great deal about Russian music, and I was very much gratified to find that these gifted young musicians were well acquainted with our music, and very sympathetically disposed towards Glinka, Balakirev, Rimsky-Korsakov, Borodin, and Glazounov. They were particularly fond of Balakirev's *Islamey*, and considered this work, on account of its originality, quite unique of its kind. On this memorable day I first heard Halir play my concerto. It appeared to me that this artist, who is endowed with wonderful beauty of tone, prodigious technique, passion, brilliancy, and power, must soon take one of the first places among the violinists of our time.

IX

After these two great days in my life I spent a whole week in Leipzig, and afterwards I twice returned there for a few days at a time. That I may not have to take up the subject of Leipzig again, I will now mention some interesting acquaintances whom I made there, and other facts of interest.

The Opera of Leipzig is proud of its gifted young conductor, Nikisch, who is a specialist as regards the later Wagner dramas. There I heard *Rheingold* —the first of the famous tetralogy—and *Meistersinger*. The orchestra of the Opera is the same as that of the Gewandhaus, and consequently first-rate; but as their playing at the concerts under Reinecke is not beyond reproach, it is evident that we can only form some idea of the perfection to which they can attain under a talented conductor by hearing their rendering of Wagner's elaborate scores when conducted by such an astonishing master of his business as Nikisch. His conducting has nothing in common with the effective and, in its way, inimitable conducting of Hans von Bülow. In proportion as the latter was mobile, restless, and showy in his style of conducting, which appealed to the eye, Herr Nikisch is elegantly calm, sparing of superfluous movements, yet at the same time wonderfully strong and self-possessed. He does not seem to conduct, but rather to exercise some mysterious spell ; he hardly makes a sign, and never tries to call attention to himself, yet we feel that the great orchestra, like an instrument in the hands of a wonderful master, is completely and irresponsibly under the control of its chief. And this chief is a somewhat short, pale, young man, about thirty years of age, with beautiful bright eyes, and gifted—it must surely be—with some magic power which makes the orchestra resound like a thousand trumpets of Jericho, or coo like a dove, or die away in a mysterious whisper. And all this is done in such a way that the audience do not notice the little conductor who is quietly ruling his obedient slave—the orchestra.

Nikisch is a Germanised Hungarian ; I imagine this is not a unique example. But certainly, among musicians at least, I never met but one who, having been born in Florence and spent his youth there, had so entirely lost the characteristic southern features (I speak from a musical point of view) of his native land, and had so completely borrowed from the Germans their language, customs, and above all their musical style, as the talented Ferrucio Busoni, with whom I became somewhat intimately acquainted. Busoni was still young when he came to live in Germany, where he attended a good music school and became a pianist of marvellous technique. I heard a quartet which Busoni had recently composed excellently played by Herr Petri's quartet. This work proved that Busoni has a decided gift for composition and also serious tendencies ; and as I have reason to believe, from personal knowledge, that the young composer has strength of character, brilliant intellect, and lofty ambitions, I have no doubt that he will soon be much talked of. For my part I listened to this quartet, and while delighting in the exceedingly original rhythmic and harmonic combinations, I could not but regret that Busoni in every way did violence to his nature, and strove, apparently, to be German at any price. Something similar may be observed in another Italian of the new generation, Sgambati. Both of them seem ashamed of being Italian ; they seem to fear lest their compositions should show a shadow of melody, and desire to make them obscure, in the German style. A sad phenomenon indeed ! That inspired old man Verdi opened out a new path to Italian composers in *Aïda* and *Otello*, without in the least imitating the German style (although some suppose, quite wrongly, that Verdi is following in Wagner's footsteps) ; while those of his young compatriots who tend towards Germany are striving to win their laurels in the land of Beethoven and Schumann at the price of doing violence to their nature. They strive to be like Brahms, deep, obscure, even wearisome, if only they may not be confounded with that host of Italian composers who, even in these days, still continue dishing up in every

style the old operatic commonplaces of Bellini and
Donizetti. But they forget that the sheep remains
a sheep in spite of the lion's skin ; and if the lion is
endowed by nature with his share of beauty and
strength, the sheep, too, is gentle, and has his
wonderful warm fleece, as well as other virtues which
should be cultivated, perfected, and valued no less
highly than the opposite qualities and merits of the
lion. I am firmly convinced that Italian music will
only enter on a new period of prosperity when, in-
stead of quarrelling with their national tendencies
and joining the ranks of the Wagnerians, Lisztites,
Brahmsites, etc., they begin to draw fresh musical
elements from the bosom of their national genius,
and, discarding the trivialities of the thirties, create
new forms in the spirit of their nationality and in
conformity with their surroundings and gorgeous
southern scenery. For the brilliant natural characteristics of the Italians, their richness of melody,
and the facile external beauty which belong to the
genius of Italian music are not perhaps incompatible
with a certain depth, though of a different kind to
that of the Germans. Busoni is an excellent pianist,
and it is very desirable that he should visit us in the
immediate future ; in any case he is a striking and
interesting personality.

To complete my impressions and experiences
of Leipzig, I will relate one interesting episode
which tends to prove that politics do not influence
music, and that Mars and Apollo, being gods, are
not jealous of each other. Since Bismarck made

his celebrated inflammatory speech in February, all Germany has been enveloped in a flame of fierce Russophobism. However, early one morning I was awakened by a noise and bustle in the corridor of my hotel, which was soon followed by a knock at my door. Somewhat alarmed, I jumped out of bed, opened the door, and learned from the waiter who was knocking that an aubade was about to begin under my window, and that politeness demanded that I should appear there, in spite of the unusual severity of the frost. The waiter then handed me a programme, elegantly designed, consisting of eight numbers of very varied music. At this moment the strains of our National Hymn resounded from below. As soon as I was dressed I opened the window and beheld in the small courtyard of the hotel, stationed immediately under my windows, a full military band, in the midst of which stood the band-master in a uniform as resplendent as that of a field-marshal. All eyes were turned towards me. I bowed, and remained standing bareheaded in the bitter frost of this early February morning. It was the band of one of the regiments then stationed in Leipzig ; an excellent one too, and they played their programme very well, which was the more surprising, because the cold was enough to paralyse the fingers of the poor musicians, who endured the cruel winter frost for over an hour. The conductor, Herr Jahrow, did me the honour of being particularly fond of my music, and, thanks to this, a body of Germans, in full uniform, had been compelled to flatter my ears that

morning.   After the serenade was finished, the conductor came up to see me, gave me a cordial greeting,
and then hastened away to his military duties.
Needless to say, I was very much touched by this
expression of sentiment.   I do not know if the other
visitors in the hotel were equally gratified at being
roused from their beds at such an early hour by the
strains of trumpets and trombones ; but at least their
curiosity must have been aroused.   From all the
windows people in various stages of costume looked
out to see what was going on.

X

THERE are two distinct symphony societies in Hamburg. One is old-established, possesses large funds and a very celebrated orchestra. The other has been started quite recently by a well-known Hamburg concert-agent, Pollini. It has no orchestra of its own, but employs the band of the Opera, which consists of second-rate artists, who are, moreover, overworked to the last degree by their service at the theatre. Both societies give a series of symphony concerts, and the Philharmonic has long since been conducted by Dr. Bernuth, an excellent and experienced conductor, who is generally respected in Hamburg both as a musician and as a very amiable and charming man. The orchestra of the other society is conducted by Hans von Bülow. As invariably happens, there exists between these two musical enterprises a deep enmity, a mutual antagonism and desire to outdo each other in receipts, success, and fame. I had been invited to conduct three of my works at one of the concerts of the Philharmonic Society, and thus fell into the camp which was opposed to Hans von Bülow, who, it seemed to me, cherished no great friendship for the Philharmonic. I felt that I was placed in an awkward position. Hans von Bülow had, in time past, done me invaluable service, and I considered myself for ever in his debt. Therefore, realising the situation of musical affairs in Hamburg, I was grieved to think that I might cause him any annoyance. But my anxiety was quite unnecessary. Hans von Bülow, being a born gentleman, took my appearance at the concert of the opposition society in a most gentlemanly way. In spite of ill-health, and extreme fatigue caused by the constant travelling from Hamburg to Bremen, Bremen to Berlin, and back again to Hamburg, which he continued to do all through the three years during which he conducted the Subscription Symphony Concerts, von Bülow accorded me a most hearty welcome. He came to call upon me, and what still more attracted the attention of all the Hamburgers, he remained from beginning to end of the concert in which I took part.

As at the first rehearsal at the Gewandhaus, I felt exceedingly nervous when on the 17th of January I attended the rehearsal at Covent Garden, the room in which the concerts of the Hamburg Philharmonic Society take place. My method of procedure with the orchestra was just the same as at Leipzig. I began with the *Finale* of my *Third Suite* (Theme and Variations). The faces of the players at the moment of my first beat expressed nothing further than a rather cool curiosity, but soon some of them began to smile and nod to each other as much as to say,

"This Russian bear is not really so very bad." A bond of sympathy was established between us, and all my agitation and diffidence vanished as though at the touch of some magic wand. The subsequent rehearsals and the concert itself brought me nothing but pleasure. Such anxiety is only unbearable when an artist is not sufficiently at home in his business, and feels himself a stranger in an entirely new sphere. These fears and agitations which every one goes through— especially a nervous man—before appearing in public, will cease to trouble him if he can believe in the sympathy of his colleagues and those around him. At the second rehearsal I experienced a rare delight at the success which fell to the lot of our young compatriot Sapellnikov. This young artist had been invited at the recommendation of Madame Sophie Menter (in whose class he had finished his course at the Conservatoire of St. Petersburg) to play, under my conductorship, my difficult *Pianoforte Concerto*, No 1.

On the eve of my departure from Petersburg I had occasion to hear Sapellnikov's playing ; and although I had been able to form some slight appreciation of its fine quality, yet—owing, perhaps, to the bustle and haste which precedes a long journey—I did not at the time observe all the rare qualities possessed by this sympathetic young pianist. Now, at the rehearsal, as Sapellnikov surmounted one after another the inconceivable difficulties of my concerto, and gradually revealed all the power and distinctiveness of his colossal gift, my enthusiasm increased, and, what was still more

the amiable Herr D. Rather, whose family have long been living in this town—ever since the death of a dear son in Petersburg, and the consequent anxiety as to the health of his remaining children, induced Herr Rather to separate himself from his family, whom he visits occasionally for three months at a time. I spent many pleasant hours with Rather, his wife, and his charming children, of whom, unfortunately, only the eldest knows a few words of Russian, although they were born in Russia. I should like to take this opportunity of declaring my deep gratitude to Herr Rather for his unceasing kindness and the friendly part he played on my behalf; for to his initiative I owe my invitation to Hamburg, and from Hamburg date all the flattering invitations which reached me, one after another, from various places in Germany.

XI

In Hamburg, as in Leipzig, I made some very interesting acquaintances. First of all I must mention the head of the committee of the Philharmonic Society, a very old gentleman, Herr Ave-Lallement. This venerable old man of over eighty paid me great attention, and gave me the flattering reception of a compatriot. In spite of his age, his infirmity, and the great distance at which he lived, Herr Lallement attended two rehearsals, the concert, and the party at Dr. Bernuth's. He carried his amiability so far as to desire to possess my photograph, taken by the best photographer in Hamburg; came to see me in person in order to ask about it, and himself arranged the hour of the sitting and the size and style of the picture. I visited the kindly old gentleman, who, as the reader can see for himself, was quite free from the prejudices of old age against all that is modern, and I had a long and very interesting chat with him. Herr Lallement candidly confessed that many of my works which had been performed in Hamburg were not at all to his mind; that he could not endure my noisy instrumentation, and disliked some of the orchestral effects to which I had recourse, especially my use of the instruments of percussion; but, for all that, he thought I had in me the making of a really good German composer. Almost with tears in his eyes he besought me to leave Russia and settle permanently in Germany, where classical conventions and the traditions of high culture could not fail to correct my faults, which were easily explicable to his mind by the fact of my having been born and educated in a country so unenlightened and, as regards progress, so far behind Germany. It was evident that he did cherish a deep prejudice against Russia, and I strove my best to overcome his hostility towards our national sentiments, of which, moreover, he was ignorant, or only knew them through the speeches of the Russophobist section. We parted good friends.

I also met with equal courtesy and amiable frankness from the leading Hamburg critic, Herr Sithardt. He attended all the rehearsals, made a close study of such of my scores as were performed, and wrote a long and detailed article, in which he censured in decisive terms the tendencies which I upheld, and found fault with my symphonic style, describing it as rough, patchy, barbarous, and suggestive of Nihilism. Herr Sithardt frankly repeated these reproaches to me in person; but at the same time his words rang with such genuine feeling, and gave evidence of such careful study and friendliness, that I preserved a very pleasant recollection of my short acquaintance with him.

Several other musicians, and people not professionally engaged in music but deeply interested in it, paid me flattering attentions, and understood how to express a cordial sympathy, leaving an ineffaceable impression upon my memory. Such were Dr. Riemann, who has devoted himself to the study of musical theory, and is not unknown to us in Russia; that witty old man Gurlitt, the composer of a number of well-known piano fantasias and transcriptions; the talented violinist Willy Burmeister; the conductor Laube, appointed to the Pavlovsk concerts in the summer of 1888; the violinists Morvege and Behr; Armbrust the organist, and many others.

From my conversation with all these, I gathered that nowhere was the Brahms cult more extensive than in Hamburg. The question of this composer's position, which was always troubling me, met with the same response here as elsewhere. Only in Hamburg I finally realised how an artist's work may sometimes be valued not for its intrinsic worth, for itself alone, but for some fortuitous reason. As our Russian proverb admirably expresses it: "When there is no fish the crayfish passes for one." The fact is that Wagner and Wagnerism does not suffice the entire German public, as many believe. No doubt there are fully convinced, energetic, and powerful advocates of Wagner, who strive in every way to establish his creed in Germany and

to further the progress of his music; but the great
mass of the German public are intensely conservative
and ready to protest against every kind of musical
innovation.   If, to a certain extent, they are reconciled to Wagner's triumph in the domain of
opera, yet in the concert-room they stand firmly by
classical tradition.   The school of Liszt, which would
like to monopolise the concert platforms, meets with
incredible obstacles and has no success.   Musical
Germans who are not infected with Wagnerism, and
hold aloof from his exclusiveness, possess a certain
modesty and a nice ear which makes them turn in
disgust from all violent effects, from all that is
decided, eccentric, piquant, brilliant, singular; in a
word, from everything that scintillates in the new
symphonic music of all the European schools.   So
strong is the need of a musician who will devote
himself to symphony in the classical style, to the
sober and recognised traditions of the great masters,
that for the lack of a new genius capable of leading
the German school in the path indicated by Haydn,
Mozart, Beethoven, Mendelssohn, and Schumann,
and their compeers, the Germans — at least the
majority of them — have concentrated their hopes
on Brahms, who, if he cannot be Beethoven, is at
least inspired by a noble ambition to follow in his
steps.

XII

THE Berlin Philharmonic Society, or I should rather
say the society of instrumentalists who hire the room
known as the " Philharmonia," invited me to attend
an extra concert consisting entirely of my own
compositions. I have already stated that the arrange-
ment of the programme was attended with some
difficulties, because Herr Schneider, the president of
the society, was anxious to perform something which
would bring me into favour with the Berlin public.
I considered, and still consider, my *Overture 1812*
quite mediocre, having only a patriotic and local significance which made it unsuitable for any but Russian
concert-rooms. But it was precisely this overture
that Herr Schneider wished to include in the programme, saying that it had been performed several
times in Berlin with success. On the other hand, I
thought that my *Romeo and Juliet* fantasia ought
to be the chief item on the programme, and Herr
Schneider, who is a very charming and amiable man,
finally agreed to this, but very unwillingly. He
thought it would be a great risk to perform such a

difficult work, which, in his opinion, was not likely to please. I decided to consult Hans von Bülow, who was well acquainted with my music as well as with the tastes of the Berlin public, and to my great surprise he sided with Herr Schneider. I then gave in.

The orchestra of the Berlin Philharmonic Society is very fine, and has what I must call the quality of elasticity, the power of stretching itself to the dimensions of a Berlioz or Liszt orchestra, and of rendering to perfection the capricious effects of Berlioz, or the massive, sonorous tones of Liszt's orchestra; while, on the other hand, it can contract to the requirements of a Haydn. In this respect the Berlin orchestra reminds me very much of those of our capital towns. This probably is due to the fact that in Berlin, as with us, a decided eclecticism dominates the concert programmes. Here, as in Petersburg or Moscow, you may hear at one concert Haydn and Glazounov, Beethoven and Bizet, Glinka and Brahms, and thus everything is executed with the same loving care, brilliancy, and *ensemble*. The musicians who are members of the Philharmonic Society are not employed at the Opera; consequently they are not tired out. Besides which, they form an association, the members of which are on an equal footing, and play for their own benefit and not for that of an agent, who pays a very small salary. This is the reason why their performances are strong and full of expression. From the very first rehearsal I was encouraged by the gentlemen of the orchestra, and by their attention and affability, and everything went off well. The rehearsal was attended by many prominent musical people, who expressed their interest in every possible way. Among them I must mention Grieg, who had purposely come from Leipzig to be at my concert, Moritz Moskovsky, Professor Ehrlich, and Hans von Bülow himself, who, in spite of extreme fatigue, appeared at the first rehearsal and was most kind to me. In spite of very unfavourable weather, the concert attracted a large audience and went off very brilliantly. Siloti played my concerto very finely, and had a great success; Sapellnikov was so good and amiable that he undertook to accompany the singer Friede, who sang several of my songs. Of the symphonic works, the *Overture 1812* and the Introduction and Fugue from my *First Suite* pleased best. I was received with loud applause.

My reader will perhaps observe that I speak less willingly and give fewer details of my visit to Berlin than might be expected, seeing its importance as the capital of Germany, but I have a reason, which I will explain. The fact is that it is difficult and painful to speak of Berlin. In my heart I still have a lively recollection of the irreparable loss which befell me in the death of the late J. I. Koteka, my pupil, and afterwards my most intimate friend, who lived in Berlin for eight years, and held a high position in the town. Every day I came in contact with people among whom the dead man had lived; many of them, like myself, were attached to him by ties of friendship; every moment I was discussing circumstances and events which keenly reminded me of my departed friend, and reopened a wound that was scarcely healed. Time alone can soften such a blow ; and it needs a long, long time to reconcile us to the death of a gifted young man full of strength and energy. . . .

Among those who were especially friendly to me in Berlin I will mention the well-known concert-agent Wolff ; the fine violinist Emil Sauret ; the celebrated Moritz Moskovsky, whose personality seemed to me as interesting as his creative gift ; the publisher and charming man Hugo Bock ; and finally Madame Artôt—so well remembered by the Moscow public. This talented singer had been living for some time in Berlin, where she was particularly appreciated and loved by the Court and the public, and where she sang with great success and also gave lessons. I was invited, together with Grieg, to spend an evening at Madame Artôt's house, the memory of which will never be effaced. Both the personality and the art of this singer are as irresistibly fascinating as ever.

LIST OF WORKS

Op. 1. No 1. Scherzo à la russe. 2. Impromptu. Two pianoforte pieces dedicated to Nicholas Rubinstein.

Op. 2. Three pieces for pianoforte. Souvenir de Hapsaal. 1. Ruines d'un Château. 2. Scherzo. 3. Chant sans paroles.

Op. 3. The Voievoda : an opera of which only two numbers exist. 1. Overture. 2. Entr'acte and Air de Ballet.

Op. 4. Valse Caprice. For pianoforte (D major).

Op. 5. Romance. For pianoforte (F minor). Dedicated to Mlle. Désirée Artôt.

Op. 6. Six songs. For voice and pianoforte.

Op. 7. Valse-Scherzo (A major). For pianoforte. Dedicated to Madame A. Davidov.

Op. 8. Capriccio (G sharp major). For pianoforte. Dedicated to C. Klindworth.

Op. 9. Three pieces for pianoforte. 1. Rêverie. 2. Polka de Salon. 3. Mazurka de Salon.

Op. 10. Two pieces for pianoforte. 1. Nocturne. 2. Humoresque.

Op. 11. First String Quartet (D major). For two violins, viola, and violoncello. Dedicated to M. Serge Ratschinsky.

Op. 12. The Snow Maiden (Snegourotchka). Music to a fairytale by Ostrovsky. 1. Introduction. 2. Dance and Chorus of Birds. 3. Monologue of the Frosts. 4. Carnival Chorus. 5. Melodrama. 5a. Entr'acte. 6. Lel's Song. 7. Lel's Song. 8. Entr'acte. 9. Chorus of Blind Gussleeplayers. 10. Melodrama. 11. Folk Chorus and Chorus of the Courtiers. 12. Choral Dance of Maidens. 13. Jesters' Dance. 14. Lel's Song. 14a. Lel's Song. 15. Brussilio's Song. 16. Appearance of the Wood Demons and the Shadow of the Snow Maiden. 17. Entr'acte. 18. March of the King of Berendei and Chorus. 19. Finale.

Op. 13. First Symphony (G minor), "Winter Day Dreams." 1. Allegro tranquillo : "Dreams on the High-road in Winter." 2. Adagio cantabile : Dreary Land, Land of Mists. 3. Allegro scherzando giocoso. 4. Finale : Andante lugubre.

Op. 14. Vakoula the Smith. Opera written for a prize competition organised by the Grand Duchess Helena, afterwards rewritten and published as The Caprices of Oxane.

Op. 15. Triumphal Overture on the Danish National Hymn. For full orchestra.

Op. 16. Six songs.

Op. 17. Second Symphony (C minor), on Malo-Russian Themes. 1. Andante sostenuto. 2. Andantino marziale. 3. Scherzo. 4. Finale.

Op. 18. The Tempest (F minor). Orchestra-fantasia on Shakespeare's play. Dedicated to M. Vladimir Stassov.

Op. 19. Six pieces for pianoforte. 1. Rêverie du Soir. 2. Scherzo humoristique. 3. Feuillet d'Album. 4. Nocturne. 5. Capriccioso. 6. Thème original et variations.

Op. 20. The Swan Lake. Ballet in four acts.

Op. 21. Six pieces for pianoforte, on one theme. Dedicated to Anton Rubinstein.

Op. 22. Second String Quartet (F major). For two violins, viola, and violoncello.

Op. 23. Concerto for pianoforte and orchestra (B flat minor). Dedicated to Hans von Bülow.

Op. 24. Eugene Oniegin. An opera in three acts. Libretto adapted from the poem of A. Poushkin.

Op. 25. Six songs. Published by V. Bessel and Co., St. Petersburg.

Op. 26. Sérénade mélancholique (B minor). For violin and orchestra. Dedicated to Herr L. Auer.

Op. 27. Six songs.

Op. 28. Six songs.

Op. 29. The Third Symphony (D major). 1. Introduction and Allegro. 2. Alla tedesca. 3. Andante elegiaco. 4. Finale : Allegro con fuoco (tempo di polacca).

Op. 30. Third String Quartet (E flat). For two violins, viola, and violoncello. Dedicated to the memory of F. Laub.

Op. 31. Slavonic March. On national themes. For full orchestra.

Op. 32. Francesca di Rimini. Orchestral fantasia from Dante's *Inferno*. Dedicated to M. Serge Taneiev.

Op. 33. Variations sur un thème rococo (7 variations and coda). For violoncello, with orchestral accompaniment. Dedicated to M. G. Fitzenhagen.

Op. 34. Valse-Scherzo (C major). For violin and orchestra.

Op. 35. Concerto (D major). For violin and orchestra. Dedicated to Mr. A. Brodsky.

Op. 36. The Fourth Symphony (F minor). For full orchestra. Dedicated "to my best friend." 1. Andante sostenuto. 2. Andantino in modo di canzone. 3. Scherzo. 4. Finale : Allegro con fuoco.

Op. 37. Grand Sonata (G major). For pianoforte. Dedicated to Herr C. Klindworth.

Op. 37a. The Seasons. Twelve characteristic pieces for pianoforte.

Op. 38. Six songs, with pianoforte accompaniment.

Op. 39. Children's Album. Twenty-four easy pieces in the style of Schumann, for pianoforte.

Op. 40. Twelve pieces for pianoforte (medium difficulty). 1. Etude. 2. Chanson triste. 3. Marche funèbre. 4. Mazurka. 5. Mazurka. 6. Chant sans paroles. 7. Au Village. 8. Valse. 9. Valse. 10. Danse russe. 11. Scherzo. 12. Rêverie interrompue.

Op. 41. The Liturgy of St. John of Chrysostom. For four voices (soprano, alto, tenor, and bass), with pianoforte accompaniment.

Op. 42. Three pieces for violin, with pianoforte accompaniment : Souvenir d'un lieu cher. 1. Méditation. 2. Scherzo. 3. Mélodie.

Op. 43. First Orchestral Suite. 1. Introduction and Fugue. 2. Divertimento. 3. Intermezzo. 4. Scherzo. 5. Gavotte.

Op. 44. Second Concerto for pianoforte and orchestra. Dedicated to Nicholas Rubinstein.

Op. 45. Capriccio italien. For orchestra.

Op. 46. Six duets. For two voices and pianoforte accompaniment.

Op. 47. Seven songs, with pianoforte accompaniment.

Op. 48. Serenade for string orchestra.

Op. 49. The Year 1812. A solemn overture, written for the opening of the Cathedral of Christ the Redeemer, Moscow.

Op. 50. Trio for piano, violin, and violoncello. Dedicated "to the memory of a great artist" (Nicholas Rubinstein).

Op. 51. Six pieces for pianoforte. 1. Valse de Salon. 2. Polka peu dansante. 3. Menuetto scherzoso. 4. Natha-Valse. 5. Romance. 6. Valse sentimentale.

Op. 52. Russian Service (first vespers). An attempt to harmonise the church canticles (for mixed choir).

Op. 53. Second Orchestral Suite. 1. Jeu de sons. 2. Valse. 3. Scherzo burlesque. 4. Rêves d'enfant. 5. Danse baroque (style Dargomijsky).

Op. 54. Sixteen songs for young people, with pianoforte accompaniment.

Op. 55. Third Orchestral Suite. 1. Elégie. 2. Valse Mélancholique. 3. Scherzo. 4. Tema con variazoni (12 variations).

Op. 56. Concert-Fantasia. For piano, with orchestral accompaniment. Dedicated to Madame Sophie Menter.

Op. 57. Six songs, with pianoforte accompaniment.

Op. 58. Manfred. Symphony, in four tableaux, from the dramatic poem by Byron. Dedicated to M. Mily Balakirev. 1. Lento lugubre : Manfred in the Alps. 2. Vivace con spirito : The Spirit of the Alps appears to Manfred. 3. Andante con moto : Pastorale. 4. Allegro con fuoco : The palace of Arimane. Manfred amid the bacchanalian revels. Evocation of the shade of Astarte. She predicts the end of his mortal woes. Death of Manfred.

Op. 59. Dumka. Russian rustic scene. For pianoforte.

Op. 60. Twelve songs, with pianoforte accompaniment. Dedicated to Her Majesty the Tsaritsa.

Op. 61. Fourth Orchestral Suite (Mozartiana). 1. Gigue. 2.

Menuet. 3. Preghicra. 4. Theme and Variations (10 variations).

Op. 62. Pezzo Capriccioso. Morceau de Concert. For violoncello, with orchestral or pianoforte accompaniment.

Op. 63. Six songs, with pianoforte accompaniment. Dedicated to His Imperial Highness the Grand Duke Constantine.

Op. 64. The Fifth Symphony (E minor). Dedicated to M. Ave-Lallement of Hamburg. 1. Andante: Allegro con anima. 2. Andante cantabile. 3. Valse: Allegro moderato. 4. Finale: Andante maestoso: Allegro vivace (alla breve).

Op. 65. Six melodies to French words.

Op. 66. Sleeping Beauty. A ballet preceded by a prologue (30 numbers).

Op. 67. Hamlet. Overture-Fantaisie for full orchestra. Dedicated to Edward Grieg.

Op. 67a. Hamlet. Overture, melodramas, marches, and entr'actes. For small orchestra.

Op. 68. Dame de Pique (Queen of Spades). An opera in three acts and seven scenes.

Op. 69. Iolanthe. A lyric opera in one act.

Op. 70. Souvenir de Florence. Sextet for stringed instruments. 1. Allegro con spirito. 2. Adagio cantabile. 3. Allegro moderato. 4. Allegro vivace.

Op. 71. Casse-Noisette (The Nut-cracker). Fairy ballet for orchestra, in two acts (15 numbers).

Op. 71a. Suite for full orchestra, adapted from the score of the Casse-Noisette ballet. 1. Overture Miniature. 2. Danses caractéristiques: (a) Marche; (b) Danse de la Fée Dragée; (c) Danse russe, Trépak; (d) Danse arabe; (e) Danse chinoise; (f) Danse des mirlitons. 3. Valse des fleurs.

Op. 72. Seventeen pieces for pianoforte.

Op. 73. Six songs, with pianoforte accompaniment.

Op. 74. Sixth Symphony, "Pathetic" (B minor). Dedicated to M. Vladimir Davidov. 1. Adagio: Allegro non troppo. 2. Allegro con grazia. 3. Allegro molto vivace. 4. Finale: Adagio lamentoso.

Op. 75. Concerto No. 3 (posthumous). For piano and orchestra. Dedicated to M. Louis Diemer.

Works without Opus Number

Romeo and Juliet. Overture-fantasia after Shakespeare, for full orchestra. Dedicated to M. Mily Balakirev.

Romeo and Juliet. Duet (soprano and tenor). Posthumous work, completed from sketches left by the composer, and orchestrated by S. Taneiev.

Elegy in memory of J. Samarin. For string orchestra.

Solemn Coronation March. For orchestra. Composed for the coronation of the Emperor Alexander III. at Moscow.

Solemn Marche. For full orchestra (posthumous).

Military March. For military band. Dedicated to the 98th Regiment of Infantry.

Impromptu—Caprice. For pianoforte.

Valse-Scherzo. For pianoforte.

Impromptu. Published in the album of old students of the Conservatoire dedicated to A. Rubinstein, St. Petersburg, 1889.

Impromptu (Momento lirico). For pianoforte (posthumous).

Perpetuum mobile. Finale of Weber's Sonata in A flat minor, arranged for left hand only.

Five songs, with pianoforte accompaniment (published separately).

Hommage à A. Rubinstein. Chorus à capella, composed for his Jubilee, 1889. Words by Polonsky.

Chorus for male voices. Dedicated to the students of Moscow University.

Chorus (The Nightingale). For mixed choir.

Night. Vocal quartet. Music arranged from Mozart's Fantasia for Piano (No. 4).

Love and Nature. Vocal trio (posthumous).

Nine church choruses for mixed voices.

Hymn in honour of SS. Cyril and Methodius. Chorus à capella on an old Slavonic melody.

Mazeppa. Opera in three acts.

Moscow. Cantata for solo, chorus, and orchestra. Written for the Coronation of the Emperor Alexander III.

The Oprichnik. Opera in four acts. Published by W. Bessel and Co., St. Petersburg.

Joan of Arc.   Opera in four acts.

The Enchantress (Charodeïka).   Opera in four acts.

Le caprice d' Oxane (Cherevichek) : Two little Shoes.   Originally published as Vakoula the Smith.

Recent Posthumous Works

Overture to the Drama *The Storm*, by Ostrovsky.   Composed in 1865.   Published by M. Belaiev, Leipzig, 1896.

Fatum (Destiny).   Symphonic poem.   Composed in 1869.   Belaiev, Leipzig, 1896.

Op. 78. The Voievoda.   Symphonic ballad.   For orchestra.   Belaiev, Leipzig, 1897.

Op. 79. Andante and Finale.   For piano and orchestra.   Instrumentation by S. Taneiev.

Except where it is otherwise stated, the works are published by
P. Jurgenson, Moscow.

THE END

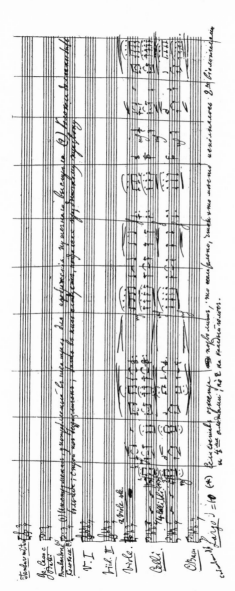

OPENING BARS FROM THE OVERTURE "1812."

From the MS. in the possession of P. Turgenson, Moscow.